IT'S YOUR CALL

WITH MORE THAN 20 POSSIBLE ENDINGS

Disney

TRON

LEGACY

INITIATE SEQUENCE

REAR VIEW DS GUNNER

IT'S YOUR CALL

WITH MORE THAN 20 POSSIBLE ENDINGS

Disney

TRON

LEGACY

INITIATE SEQUENCE

Written by Carla Jablonski
Based on the screenplay written by Eddy Kitsis & Adam Horowitz
Based on characters created by Steven Lisberger and Bonnie MacBird
Executive Producer Donald Kushner
Produced by Sean Bailey, Jeffrey Silver, Steven Lisberger
Directed by Joseph Kosinski

Disney PRESS
New York

Printed in the United States of America

First Edition
1 3 5 7 9 10 8 6 4 2
J689-1817-1-10244

Library of Congress Catalog Card Number on file.
ISBN 978-1-4231-3601-9
Visit www.disneybooks.com

In your hands you hold an object of great power. It has the ability to alter the course of history. The choices YOU make with this item will impact moments in time, fateful events, and could even mean the difference between life and death for those closest to you.

As Sam, will you grab hold of your father's legacy and become a hero to many in a digital world beyond imagining? OR will you turn your back on his dreams and end up living an ordinary life in the real world? These and countless other choices are yours to make. Will you initiate a new game?

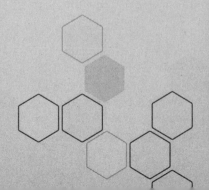

IT'S YOUR CALL.

PROLOGUE

You are Sam Flynn, son of the brilliant computer genius Kevin Flynn. He became a billionaire by inventing new technology, awesome software programs, and video games galore. In fact, he created one of the most popular games of all time: Tron. Then, when you were seven years old, he disappeared.

At first there was a lot of speculation: was he in seclusion working on his next great digital breakthrough? Was there foul play? Or was it something much less interesting, but far more upsetting—he simply abandoned you?

That was twenty years ago.

You had stopped thinking about all this a long time before. You never cared about Encom, the multibillion-dollar company you inherited. You just let the CEOs handle it. You don't bother showing up at board meetings or putting in any time at company headquarters.

Except once a year.

Once a year you make a very unconventional appearance. You perform a crazy, risky, stomach-dropping stunt. And you just pulled off another doozy.

TURN TO PAGE 2

You grin as you hurtle along the dark streets on your motorcycle, heading for home. This year's prank totally rocked. The expressions on everyone's faces as you leaped off the top of the Encom skyscraper? Priceless! Adrenaline still pumps through your veins as you remember the swan dive . . . the *whoosh* of the air . . . the sudden snap of the parachute as it opened.

You're seriously stoked. Even that little brush with the cops when you landed was completely worth it.

You cruise through a junkyard near the docks. A series of large shipping containers sits on a barge accessible from the wharf. That's where you're heading.

You park your bike. "Home sweet home," you announce as you enter through a garage door and step into your shipping-container apartment.

Marv, your dog and closest friend, barks a greeting. You absentmindedly kick the crumpled ghee-and-yellow belt out of your way as you cruise by the mats you have set out for your martial-arts training sessions.

Flopping down on the sofa, you stretch out. You glance at your father's classic motorcycle up on blocks in a corner. "Really need to finish that rebuild job," you mutter.

Marv suddenly starts barking. You look up to discover a man standing in the doorway.

TURN TO PAGE 3

The man is Alan Bradley. You've known him your whole life. Before your dad pulled his famous vanishing act, Alan was his business partner.

"What are you doing in my apartment?" you ask.

"You don't answer your phone," Alan replies simply. "How have you been?"

You roll your eyes. "You know, when I was twelve I might've appreciated the whole surrogate-father thing. But come on, Alan. I got it all under control now."

He eyes your messy apartment and your stunt-disheveled appearance. "Clearly," he says drily.

Alan walks to the large window at the front of your apartment and gazes across the river at the illuminated Encom building. "Nice view," he comments. "Heard you just did a triple axle off her."

When you don't respond, he continues. "Also heard you sent the last batch of dividend checks to some interesting causes."

You scratch Marv's ears. "The dog park? That was Marv's idea." You sigh and look at Alan. "Are we going to do this again? Really? Do I look like I'm ready to run a Fortune 500 company?"

"No," Alan says. "And the board is pretty happy with you staying out of things. But I must say, you sure have an interesting way of being disinterested."

Enough small talk. "Why are you here, Alan?" you repeat.

TURN TO PAGE 4

4

Alan's expression becomes more serious. "I promised you if I ever got any information about your dad, I'd tell you first."

You stare at him, stunned, as he pulls out an old-fashioned pager.

"I got a page last night," he explains. "From the arcade. A number that's been disconnected for twenty years."

This is too weird. Suddenly you feel all fidgety.

"Two nights before he disappeared, he came to my house," Alan continues. "He was talking about genetic algorithms, quantum teleportation. He said he was about to change everything." He gazes at you, his face full of compassion. "He wouldn't have left all that. He wouldn't have left *you*."

His words rattle you, but you quickly recover. "You and I both know he's either dead or chilling in Costa Rica. Probably both." You shake your head. "I'm sorry, man. Let's do this again in a couple of years, okay?"

Alan pulls an old set of keys out of his pocket. "These are the keys to the arcade. I haven't gone over yet. I thought you should be the one."

"You're acting like I'm going to find him sitting there working," you say.

Alan grins. "Wouldn't that be something." He tosses the keys at you. You catch them out of reflex.

After he leaves, you stand gazing down at the keys, uncertain.

TURN TO PAGE 9

You stroll through the aisles of humming games, recognizing all your old favorites. Memories flash through your mind. You finger a quarter in your pocket. What should you play?

You stop in front of a game you spent hours on—Tron. You pull out the quarter and search around for the slot.

As you reach to insert the coin, it slips from your fingers. “Sheesh!” you mutter. “That’s my only one.” Dropping down to retrieve the money, you notice major scuff marks on the wood floor. It looks as if the machine has been moved—a lot. You grip its sides hard and move the game away from the wall.

Your eyes grow wide. There’s an opening hidden behind the game! You step through and find a secret stairway.

Heart pounding, you descend the narrow, dust-choked stairs. You reach the bottom and face double doors. You take a deep breath. And then you swing them wide open.

TURN TO PAGE 39

6

The guy in that ship above the court seems to be in charge. You have to convince him that there has been a big mistake.

You race across the court until you're just below the ship. You wave frantically. "Hey!" you shout. "You, up there! You need to stop this game! Yoo-hoo! Hello? Yo!"

The masked man's face tips down toward you. Great! You got his attention.

You cup your hands around your mouth, hoping he can hear you. Maybe the arena is miked? Well, no matter what, you have to try.

"I don't belong here! I'm not one of these . . ." You sweep your arm to indicate the other players. "I'm a person! I'm not from here! You have to—"

Swish! You feel the breeze of your combatant's disc as it rushes by your head. That was close.

TURN TO PAGE 98

Your heart sinks. But you can't be distracted.

The green rider on your team is up ahead. Thousands of fans whoop and cheer, eager for the action to come to them.

Clu is fast on Green's trail. You lag behind them, watching as Clu pulls up beside Green. He reaches over to Green's throttle and revs it. Your jaw drops. There are no fouls called in this game! Anything goes!

The sudden rush of speed sends Green spinning out of control toward the edge of the track. He strikes the bleachers and is sent sprawling. He derezzes when he hits the ground, and his bike flies into the stands. There's total chaos as the fans scramble to get out of the way, but it's no use. Dozens of screaming programs derezz.

Clu is ruthless, you realize.

You have to take him out.

You fall in beside him, and you both accelerate. The crowd howls excitedly. Every time Clu tries to pull ahead you match him move for move.

Wham! He rams you, sending your Light Cycle spinning toward a light wall. Just at the point of impact, you leap off the bike.

Clu bears down on you. His Light Cycle speeds up, and like a swordsman on horseback, he unsheathes his disc and prepares for the kill.

Do you fling yourself out of the way? TURN TO PAGE 15.

Do you pull out your own disc? TURN TO PAGE 44.

8

The next morning you go to the lot to see if you can find the guys. Tyler is there, and so is Luke. There's a girl with them working on Luke's bike.

"Hey!" you call as you come to a screeching halt. You hop off the bike and join them.

"What's up, man?" Tyler says.

"Looks like I'm finally going to need an actual job," you say.

"Harsh," Luke says.

"Yeah. But I thought if I could do something with bikes it wouldn't be so bad. You've seen my moves. Do you think I have a shot at stunt riding?"

Tyler narrows his eyes, studying you. "Could be." He looks over at the girl. "Hey, Jax! I've got a newbie for you!"

The girl wipes grease off her face with her T-shirt. "You want to do stunts?"

"I do," you tell her.

"This grease monkey is my sister Jax," Tyler explains. "She's a stunt coordinator on a film shooting in town."

She rattles off a list of questions. "Got nerves of steel? Good reflexes? Strong upper body?"

"I'd say yes to all three," you say.

TURN TO PAGE 26

Your hands open and close around the keys. Then you slip them into your pocket and cross to your bookshelf. Reaching out, you pick up one of the action figures on the shelf.

"Clu," you say, announcing the name of the character from one of your father's games. "Stands for 'Codified Likeness Utility.'" You shake your head and replace the figure. You remember the bedtime stories your dad used to tell—all about how he made it *inside* the computer system and back out again. They were exciting tales. Clu had been an important character in them. He had been made to look like your dad, so the action figure has your father's face—in miniature.

You dust off Tron, another figure wearing an armorlike outfit. Your dad's stories made Clu, Tron, and all the other characters seem like real people. You grin at the U-shaped vehicle known as a Recognizer. It used to serve as your night light.

You haven't looked closely at these toys in a long time. They've just always been there. You spin around and stride back to the window and stare at the blinking Encom building.

You shove your hands into your pockets and feel the keys again.

What should you do?

If you decide to go and check out the arcade,
TURN TO PAGE 16.

If you decide to forget the whole thing,
TURN TO PAGE 116.

"Huh?" you say, confused.

"Gopher. As in 'go for,'" she says. "So *go for* my coffee. When you get back, I'll need you to make some copies and fax them to the office." She strides away.

"She doesn't need any more caffeine," you mutter as you scan the area, looking for where you might find coffee. You spot a catering truck and jog toward it.

This is totally bogus, you think, kicking a rock out of your way. You wanted to use your motorcycle skills, not your ability to carry a cup of coffee. This is as bad—*worse*—than working with Encom. At least there you'd be the boss. Sort of. Even if you're not sure what that means exactly . . .

You refill the thermos and reluctantly start back across the set. You see a stunt guy who's going to handle the motorcycle trick. You seethe with envy. He's not any better than you on a bike! In fact, you've given him pointers! So unfair.

He waves you over. "Listen, I really have to go to the bathroom," he says urgently. "Can you guard the bike? I can't leave it unattended. I'll be right back."

"Sure," you tell him. He rushes away. An idea forms. . . .

You and the stunt guy are dressed alike. You're the same build. You can rock the stunt, you're sure of it.

Should you try to pull off the stunt yourself? TURN TO PAGE 38.

Or should you just watch the bike and then bring Jax her coffee. TURN TO PAGE 46.

"It's okay," you assure her. "We're safe now. We're on some kind of solar ship heading for the Portal."

Quorra takes a deep breath and releases it. "Clu has Flynn's disc?"

You nod. "Once I get out, I can shut him down."

"I should never have sent you to Zuse," she says, frowning. "That was a mistake. I should have known he might have changed."

"It's okay. I've made plenty of mistakes myself," you tell her.

"Where is your father?" she asks.

"He said he's 'knocking on the sky . . .'"

"'And listening to the sound,'" she finishes for you.

"I guess you've heard that one before," you say.

"I've heard them all. I've been with him a long time. He's changed since you've come here," she adds. "He had lost hope and now . . . Well, I haven't seen him like this in a long time. It's . . . nice."

You and Quorra stand on the deck of the solar sailer and gaze at the brilliant pillar of light signifying the Portal up ahead. "Some view," you comment.

"It's how I imagine a sunrise must be," Quorra says. "Something I've always wanted to see."

Your father suddenly stands. "Get below. Move," he orders.

TURN TO PAGE 58

You're not in the mood to try to figure out some weird game. Just being in the arcade's secret lab gives you a bad feeling. You hit **NO.**

The console begins to rumble under your hands. A high-pitched wail comes from the game speakers. It almost sounds as if the game is . . . *crying*. You could swear it's moaning "why?"

You stumble away from the desk as it rattles and shakes. "I didn't mean to insult you!" you shout. "Don't take it personally!"

You stare as the shaking grows violent and the desk starts moving toward you, tipping from side to side on its legs.

Are you actually being chased by a *computer*? All because you didn't want to play a game?

Okay, you may be losing your mind, but you still have to get out of there. It's as though you set off an earthquake! The floor buckles and cracks beneath your feet. A filing cabinet topples over, smashing onto the desk. The screen shatters, sending out flames and sparks.

You cough as acid smoke fills the room. Your eyes tear, but you make it to the stairs. There are popping sounds behind you, like firecrackers going off. You glance over your shoulder.

Oh, no! The desk is having mini-explosions! Suddenly there's a crash and a *BOOM!*

The ceiling collapses in front of you.

You're trapped. For good.

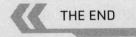

THE END

Would these programs really play against Clu? If they survive, he's bound to retaliate. You can't trust them to be truly on your side.

You set your sights on Clu. You alone have to take him out.

You gun your engine and zip toward Clu, a wall of light trailing behind you. Still, the purple and green players are closing ranks. You accelerate and zigzag in front of them. They crash into your light wall and go sprawling onto the Grid.

You hear Aqua shouting behind you, but you can't let him distract you. Your entire focus is on Clu. You're gaining on him.

Your eyes widen. Instead of trying to get away, Clu spins his bike around and heads straight toward you. What is this, a game of chicken?

You grip your handlebars hard. If you can make a sharp turn at just the right moment, he'll run into your light wall. It will be game over for—

CRASH!

You slam into one of Clu's Sentries. You were so intent on Clu that you stopped paying attention to the other players on the game grid!

You fly over the front wheel of your bike and slam onto the ground. Your bike lands on top of you. The bike crackles with flashing energy as it shorts out. Your whole body trembles as energy from the Grid shoots up through you into the bike. It feels as if you've been struck by lightning—over and over again!

The last sight you ever see is Clu looming over you with a huge grin on his face.

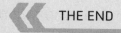

THE END

Suddenly you find yourself floating toward the ceiling! Somehow gravity has been reversed!

Your opponent is apparently not bothered by the lack of gravity. He races around while you're still trying to figure out how to move upside down. In a swift, surprise move, he knocks you to the ground—er, ceiling.

"Agghhh!" you scream as his disc slices into your arm, pinning you to the ground.

The buzzer sounds again and once more gravity changes, slamming you face-first back onto the court surface. Your visor cracks and your head spins. But at least your opponent's disc fell out, releasing you and ending the awful pain.

You stand, feeling wobbly, and look around for your opponent.

Wham! He leaps onto your back and smashes you to the ground again.

But then a strange thing happens. The guy jumps off and backs away from you. The crowd starts to boo and shout. You whirl around and see your opponent pointing at something on the court floor.

A drop of your blood.

A voice crackles down from the ship above. "Identify yourself, program!"

Should you tell them you aren't actually a program? Or will that only lead to a worse fate?

If you keep it to yourself, GO TO PAGE 114.

Or do you tell them who you are? DO THAT ON PAGE 72.

You fling yourself out of his path, somersaulting under the disc that Clu hurls at you.

He turns to gloat, then realizes you're still alive. He's so surprised, he smashes into an embankment. His own disc flies back toward him like a boomerang. As you watch, it slices into him and he derezzes.

A hush falls over the crowd. You've never heard such silence. Thousands of eyes are fixed on you.

You killed their leader. What are they going to do now?

Then a huge cheer rises up, so loud it nearly knocks you off your feet. Clu may have been the ruler, but he had more enemies than followers.

You're their hero. Practically a god to them. Thousands of grateful programs rush out of the stands.

Uh-oh.

It quickly becomes a riot as everyone wants to thank you, touch you, carry you on their shoulders, pat you on the back, shake your hand, and express their gratitude.

"Stop!" you cry, struggling to stay upright. "Wait—no!"

In all the shouting and cheering, pushing and shoving, no one notices when you fall to the ground. Which means no one helps you up. Or avoids stepping on you. Crushing you. Trampling you . . . to death.

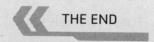

THE END

You have to check out the arcade. If nothing else, you want to find out how a message got sent from the place. The whole ride over you keep reminding yourself that your father isn't going to be there; that the page is not really a clue. It's just some random blip.

You arrive at Flynn's arcade. The whole area is rundown, and the abandoned arcade blends right in, with its boarded windows, peeling posters, and darkened neon sign.

The keys stick a little, but you manage to get inside. You haven't been here for years. Clearly, neither has anyone else. You carefully step inside the dark and dusty room.

Everything looks so much smaller. . . . The last time you were here you barely cleared the levers of the old-school pinball machines. Of course, you were seven years old at the time.

There's something spooky about the silence and the silhouettes of ghostly machines. Once your eyes have adjusted to the dark, you hurry to the circuit breakers. You flip a switch and the machines gurgle to life. Some old tune blasts from the jukebox in a corner, making you jump.

TURN TO PAGE 5

"Let's check out the games," you tell Alex. "But we're just going to watch. Not play. I bet you're good at watching."

"I'm *excellent* at watching," Alex agrees, his eyes brightening.

You and Alex head into the huge stadium. You walk around until you find an entrance. Crowds stomp and cheer above your head, so you head up a nearby ramp.

Alex rushes ahead of you, eager to see what game is being played. He comes to a sudden stop.

"What's wrong?" you ask, jogging to catch up to him.

"I think we're in the wrong place," Alex says.

You gaze around. Thousands of spectators stare back at you. You stand on a huge transparent platform that suddenly swings and latches onto another one nearby. A motorcycle zooms onto the field. Then another motorcycle zooms into place behind you.

"I think you're right," you tell Alex. "We're in the *middle* of the game!"

Now both bikes gun their engines—and head straight toward you and Alex!

TURN TO PAGE 131

18

You think your odds are a lot better if you get out of here—fast! You throw yourself into the vehicle. The driver executes a 360-degree burnout and peels away.

"Who are you?" you ask.

"Hold on," the masked driver replies.

You notice movement behind you. You whip your head around and see two grid panels flip over. They transfer two black cycles onto your level of the game grid. One of them catches up to your vehicle. Your driver swerves and knocks the black cycle into an obstacle. The cycle derezzes.

The driver flips a switch on the console and ejects a series of disc-shaped capsules. The capsules explode, knocking over the remaining black cycle and rider.

You think he's done for but watch in astonishment as he grabs a second baton off his thigh and forms a new Light Cycle beneath him. He's instantly back in pursuit!

Your driver mashes the throttle as you race toward the formidable boundary wall.

"Watch out!" you shout.

Did this driver save you from Clu just to crash you into a wall?

TURN TO PAGE 31

You'll be way too exposed on the bridge. You duck into a nearby stadium. Hopefully, the Sentries won't look for you so close by. It will be like hiding in plain sight.

You dash into what looks like a high-tech locker room. It seems safe. Nothing happening here.

"You're late!" a gruff voice hollers. "Don't just stand there! Go resupply the winks!"

Uh-oh.

You whirl around and see a stocky little guy holding what looks like a supersize vacuum cleaner glaring at you from the doorway. "I have emergency cleanup to do," he hollers. "Get the winks out there! Now!"

He rushes away. His emergency may have just saved you. He didn't even wait long enough to discover you're not who he thinks you are. You slide down onto the floor and stretch out your legs. You could seriously use a nap.

Then another person bursts into the room.

TURN TO PAGE 85

You peer across the game court. A lean, black-clad warrior steps onto the platform. His visor completely obscures his features, and his muscled body looks as if it was poured from metal. This dude was built for combat. He tosses his disc from one hand to the other almost casually.

As much as you hate it, you're going to have to fight him. To the death.

You grip your disc and bend your knees, ready to move. Your eyes widen as you watch your opponent press the center of his disc. It pops into two, one for each hand!

"Come on," you complain. "Is that even legal?"

He hurls the discs at you and you bound out of the way. The lethal weapons arc out, hit the enclosure walls, then spin back to your opponent.

You fire your disc at his head, hoping his focus is split between his returning discs and yours. But he flips into the air, twists, then lands neatly on his feet, holding his discs and successfully dodging yours.

The crowd goes wild.

"Yeah, yeah, very slick," you mutter.

Your opponent races up the side walls and you do the same, not wanting him to gain an advantage. You fire your discs simultaneously. You narrowly miss each other and tumble back down onto the platform.

You hear a loud buzzing and a deep rumble.

Now what? you wonder.

TURN TO PAGE 14

He studies you for a moment. Then he breaks out into a huge grin. "There's much to do." He gesticulates wildly as he rattles off ideas: "You'll need to change your attire. You'll need a forged disc—not easy these days, by the way—and of course you'll need transport across the Sea of Simulation." He moves across the room, away from you.

Movement outside the window catches your attention. Your eyes widen as you watch black-clad figures appear in the sky! They're actually *flying*—with the help of propellerlike wings whirring on their backs.

"Ahh, the Black Guard," Zuse says. "So prompt."

You jump to your feet and glare at Zuse. "That light change in the club," you realize. "It was a signal."

"So clever," he says. "Much like your father."

"Playing all the angles," you say with a snarl.

He just shrugs. "The game has changed, Son of Flynn."

You race toward the exit, only to discover the stairs are no longer there.

Do you try to find another way out?
TURN TO PAGE 122.

Or do you try holding Zuse hostage?
TURN TO PAGE 35.

22

You can't believe your eyes. Your *father*. Exactly as he was the day you last saw him. Exactly! He hasn't aged one bit. How is that possible?

"Sam," your father says, studying you. "Look at you, man." He grins and laughs. "How'd you get in here?"

"I-I got your message and—"

"So it's just you?" your father asks.

"Yeah . . . just me." You can't take your eyes off him. So many emotions and questions run through you. You feel as if you're about to explode or have a meltdown.

He seems to be having a similar reaction. "Wow. This is something, isn't it?"

"You look . . . the same," you say.

He smiles at you, a mischievous glint in his eyes. "A lot's happened, Sam. More than you could ever imagine." He tilts his head and addresses your game opponent. "Rinzler, the disc, please."

You stand there, puzzled, as your opponent, Rinzler, removes your disc from its sheath in your armor. He hands it to your dad, who turns away from you. What is he doing?

"Interesting," he murmurs. Then your dad turns back and tosses you back your disc. "Rinzler, Jarvis, go," he orders. Your opponent and the dark, gaunt man take off immediately, leaving you alone with your dad.

TURN TO PAGE 24

You keep walking. She works for the games, which means she works for Clu. There's no way she would help you.

You don't want her to know where you're headed, so you walk past the entrance to the giant building. You'll walk around the block and then try again once she's gone.

You round the corner—straight into a pair of Sentries.

"Identify yourself, program," one of them orders.

"Uh . . . uh . . ."

"Sounds faulty. Must be a disc problem," the other sentries says. He steps forward and holds out his hand. "Disc."

You stare at him blankly. You know that your disc reveals who you are—the son of Kevin Flynn and Clu's enemy. You don't want to just hand it over to them. The announcement you heard said that programs without ID would be deleted. But then again, how can they delete you? You're not a program. Maybe you don't need to be afraid!

"Sorry, buddy," you say, crossing your arms. "My disc is *my* business. And I'm keeping it. Haven't you heard of identity theft? You don't just hand things over to strangers!"

The Sentry is not amused.

TURN TO PAGE 76

24

The two of you stand staring at each other.

You've thought about this moment for so long—almost your whole life—and yet it's awkward and strange.

You're the first to break the silence. "You were trapped inside here," you venture. "Is that what happened?"

"That's right," he says.

"And you're in charge," you say.

He nods. "Two for two."

"So let's get out of here!" you say eagerly.

"Don't think so," he says. "Nope. Not gonna happen."

Your forehead crinkles with confusion. "But why not? What's wrong? I'm your son!"

He moves in closer, bringing his face just inches from yours. He plants his hands on your shoulders. His eyes glisten with malevolent delight. "You see, Sam, I'm not your father. But I am very, *very* happy to see you."

You gape after him as he strides out of the room.

TURN TO PAGE 61

You rush down the stairs, not even bothering to try and keep quiet. Blue smoke wafts around the room, but nothing looks damaged.

You spot a curly head bent over the computer console. At the sound of your thundering footsteps, the curly head turns around.

A kid with braces grins at you. "I got in!" he cheers. "I don't know how I did it, but I did!" He turns and stares down at the screen. "But there's nothing on the screen but a map of something called the Grid." He tries pushing some buttons. "I can't get it to do anything."

You rush over to the console. The kid is right. A digital version of the map your dad has hanging on the wall is now lit up on the screen. You're about to try fiddling with the controls when you remember why you're here.

"Who are you?" you ask the kid. "And what are you doing in here? This place has been closed for years!"

The kid shrinks into a chair. "Am I in trouble?"

You study him, trying to keep a fierce expression on your face. But the kid looks so pathetic—as if he's trying not to cry.

"Nah," you say, with a wave of your hand. "It's cool."

The kid immediately perks up. "So, do you know anything about this computer?" he asks eagerly.

TURN TO PAGE 66

A few days later you ride your motorcycle onto the movie set to report for your first day of work. It's crazy busy, with people barking into walkie-talkies, equipment being hauled, vans unloading, and actors milling around drinking coffee and bottled water.

"Hi, Jax," you say, catching sight of her familiar face.

Jax glances at you, nods, then goes back to explaining a stunt to her crew. "Got it?" she asks. The three men and two women nod and head for a motorcycle and a stunt car parked nearby.

You start to follow them.

"Where are you going?" Jax asks.

"Those are the vehicles for the stunts, right?" you say. "Just clue me in on my bit and I'm ready."

"You're not in this stunt," Jax says.

"Oh," you reply. "So you want me to prep for something else?"

"I want you to get me a coffee refill. Black, six sugars." She hands you her thermos.

"But . . . But I thought . . . What?" you sputter.

"Kid, no one starts with stunts. You work your way up, learn the ropes, get used to the set," Jax explains. "Then you get a shot. Maybe. For now, you're a gopher."

TURN TO PAGE 10

"You really should answer your phone," Alan scolds. "What's the point of technology if you don't use any of it?"

"What's so important?" you ask. You limp over to the fridge and grab a soda. Man, you could really use a long soak in a hot tub. Every muscle is screaming after the long session on your bike.

"The board of directors has forced you out, and a new owner has come in," Alan informs you. "Encom—the company your father built—is gone."

You shrug. You've had no interest in Encom from day one. You can earn your own way. That company just represents everything you despise—corporate greed, soulless guys in suits. And—oh, yeah—where your dad spent all his time. When he could have spent it with you.

"I'll be fine," you tell him. "I've got some irons in the fire." With your riding skills, you figure your motorcycle buddies can help you find some kind of gig.

TURN TO PAGE 8

"Is she going to be okay?" you ask, gazing down at Quorra.

"I don't know," your father admits, hovering over her. "I have to identify the damaged code. It's very complex."

"She risked her life for me," you say.

"Some things are worth the risk," your father says. He pats your shoulder.

He stands up and adds cryptically, "Time to knock on the sky and listen to the sound." He walks away and settles down in a quiet spot.

Quorra's eyes flutter open. She sits up and looks around, disoriented.

TURN TO PAGE 11

Bartik drags you out of the club to a dilapidated shack nearby. You try to explain who you are, but he doesn't believe you. He thinks you're using what you overheard as leverage. The questions go on and on and they just confuse you. This place is so crazy!

Then one day, a *long* time in the future, Bartik disappears! Right in front of your eyes. And in his place is Alex—all grown up!

"Sorry I took so long," Alex says. "It took a while to crack the codes." He smiles. "Time to go home."

Those are the best words you've heard in centuries.

THE END

You don't want to risk bailing without any idea of what's happening. You still have to get to the Portal. So you hurry along the huge containers, searching for a good place to hide. All of a sudden, the containers flicker to life, startling you.

Your eyes widen in shock. The lights in the translucent containers illuminate the cargo inside. And what strange cargo! Hundreds of people—*programs*, you remind yourself—are packed in together, tight as sardines.

"What is all this?" Quorra asks.

"Clu can't create programs. He can only destroy or repurpose them," your father finally answers, puzzling it out.

"Repurpose them for what?" you ask.

You sidle forward past the last of the containers and toward the edge of the ship. You look out beyond the cargo area to see the docking bay.

Cargo ships are being loaded onto what looks like an enormous aircraft carrier. The Rectifier, you realize. Tanks and other military vehicles are being fueled. You see thousands of troops gathered in formation.

"Clu is building an army!" You gasp. "That's what all these programs are for!"

TURN TO PAGE 60

Just when it looks as if you're going to crash, your mysterious driver flips another switch on the console, firing two light missiles that rip a massive hole in the wall.

Man, you think, this vehicle comes equipped with serious firepower.

The vehicle blasts through the opening. As it does, knobs grow out of the tires, turning it into an off-road vehicle.

"Made it," the driver declares with quiet triumph.

Your breath starts to return to normal. The driver turns to you as her helmet retracts on its own, revealing . . . a raven–haired beauty.

"I'm Quorra," she says.

"Uh . . . uh, thanks, Quorra." You glance in the rearview mirror and notice that the remaining driver has given up his pursuit.

"He's turning around," you say. You frown. "He's just giving up?"

"Not by choice," Quorra explains. "They can't go off-Grid. They'll lose power."

"What about us?" you ask.

Quorra smirks. "Obviously not."

"Where are you taking me?" you ask.

She guns the engine. "Patience, Sam Flynn," she says. "All your questions will soon be answered."

TURN TO PAGE 40

You didn't mean to make the kid cry. He's about eight years old and small for his age. You figure if he's hanging around abandoned arcades he probably doesn't have too many friends. Now you feel like a big bully.

"Hey," you say, trying to think of a way to at least get him up off the ground. "You did an awesome thing. I mean, you got us transported . . . into the computer, no less!"

It seems to work. "I did, didn't I!" Alex pops up again and pumps his fist in the air. "I totally rule!"

Man, this kid has serious mood swings. Were you like this when you were his age? Maybe he's been having too much sugar. . . .

"Time to explore!" he says, tugging your hand. "I have to be home before dark, so we have to get moving!"

"What are you talking about?" you ask, shaking him off. "It was already dark when I found you at the arcade."

"Oh, right." He breaks out into a big grin. "So I'm already in trouble! I can stay here as long as I want!"

His words remind you of something. You're not completely sure how you got here. So, how are you going to get back home?

TURN TO PAGE 86

A sudden lurch bangs you into the half-faced man. You recoil and regain your balance. The Recognizer has docked.

"Where are we?" you ask the young guy.

"The gaming complex," the kid replies. The nervous dude beside him amps up his muttering.

A ramp descends, and Sentries escort everyone in the hold onto the landing platform outside a gleaming superstructure. There are more Sentries waiting here, watching you all expectantly.

Your group is lined up roughly and a Sentry strolls in front of you. He nods at the kid. "Rectifier." He moves down the line. "Games," he announces in front of the muttering dude.

"Noooo," the nervous dude moans. He suddenly makes a break for it. As Sentries close in he reaches an air shaft. Without even breaking stride, he leaps into the pit. You hear his scream all the way down.

Your group is rattled, but no one says a word. The Sentries just go back to their assessment. They stop in front of you.

"Look, I know you probably get this a lot," you say, "but there's been a mistake."

The Sentry looks you up and down, then announces, "Games."

TURN TO PAGE 83

"We need to strike now," Bartik insists. "Zuse can unite the factions."

"Of course Zuse *can* do these things." Castor waves his hand dismissively. "But does he want to? We shall see. . . ."

You hear no more because at that moment Gem strides to Castor's booth. She whispers into his ear. His eyes fix on you.

"Excuse me," Castor tells Bartik. "I have to attend to something." He slides out of the booth and approaches you.

"Come!" he declares, a huge grin on his face. "Away from these primitive functions." He slides his arm over your shoulder, and slips his other arm around Gem. He escorts you through the club.

"The Son of Flynn," he says softly. "Of all the possibilities . . . and he walks into mine."

He snakes you through the dance floor and releases you. "Castor," he says, extending his hand. "Your host. Provider of any and all entertainments."

"I'm looking for Zuse," you say, not bothering to shake the guy's hand. There's something oily about him.

"This, good sir, is a conversation best had behind closed doors." He once again wraps an arm around your shoulder and drags you away.

"Change the lights," Castor orders his DJ. Instantly, the lights shift, the colors becoming even more brilliant. The rays radiate across the sky.

TURN TO PAGE 93

You leap at Zuse and knock his cane out of his hands. The momentum makes him stumble, which gives you a chance to get behind him and wrap your arm around his throat.

The Black Guard crash through the skylight.

“Back off,” you snarl, “or I’ll happily derezz him right now.”

You hope they care.

They may not, but Zuse certainly does. “False alarm!” he cries. “Terrible mistake. So sorry to have troubled you!”

They stop moving closer. But you don’t know if that will last.

“Activate the stairway,” you hiss into Zuse’s ear. You tighten your hold for emphasis.

You drag Zuse down into the pulsating club, never releasing your grip no matter how much he squirms.

How will you get this guy to help you reach the Portal?

Well, no point standing here trying to come up with a plan. You’ve got to get out of there—pronto!

TURN TO PAGE 109

Focus, Sam, you tell yourself. You have to learn the rules of this game and *fast*!

A commotion on an adjacent platform distracts you. There are players battling all around you on the multiple platforms. Crazy!

A bearded man on a nearby platform throws a disc at another player. It's a hit! The struck player's body shatters into thousands of tiny cubes that scatter across the court like shards of glass.

You should have known! They're not people! They're computer programs. And to die here is to pixilate—lose resolution. They derezz!

In this game, if you lose, you die. It's that simple.

You struggle to remove the disc from the sheath in your armor. Your combatant flings his disc again. It looks wildly off track—*phew*! But, no! It strikes a rear embankment and caroms wickedly back toward you! You drop and somersault out of its path.

Is there any hope of surviving this battle?

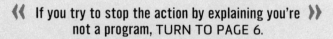

If you try to stop the action by explaining you're not a program, TURN TO PAGE 6.

If you yank out your disc to fire back, TURN TO PAGE 42.

You don't feel ready to hit the city—you want to get a better sense of where you are and of what you can expect first. "Let's check out the light show," you tell Alex.

"Awesome!" He dashes ahead and you have to jog to keep up with him.

It takes you a while to reach your destination. When you do arrive you see vibrantly colored energy that rises and falls like the waves of the ocean. No wonder it's listed on the map as the Sea of Simulation—it looks just like water. You and Alex travel along something resembling a shoreline, watching the violet and turquoise bursts.

Alex stops suddenly and kicks off his sneakers.

"What are you doing?" you ask.

"Wading!" he cries and runs toward the undulating waves of light.

You're not sure this is a good idea. What if the kid gets electrocuted or something by hurling himself into all that energy? "Alex, get back here!" you call.

Alex stops, turns, and sticks out his tongue at you.

But before he can turn back around, a shaft of light shoots down from the sky directly onto him. He's lifted off the ground and pulled up inside what looks like a giant spaceship.

It all happens so quickly, you don't have a chance to move, to gasp, or to do anything at all to save him!

TURN TO PAGE 77

38

This is my chance, you think. I'll show Jax how good I am! Then you're sure she'll find someone else to run her errands.

You pull on the helmet, making your disguise complete, and put the bike in gear. It growls to life. You pull up alongside the parked stunt car.

"CUT!" someone cries.

Uh-oh. You have a bad feeling you just made a big mistake.

"Who's the idiot who just rode into the shot?" a large man bellows through a megaphone.

You feel a pair of hands yank you off the bike. "What do you think you're doing?" the stunt rider shouts. "Why do you think I needed someone to watch the bike? So jerks like you don't ride it!"

You hang your head. "Sorry, man, I just wanted—"

Jax stalks up to you. "Off the set. Now!" she shrieks.

You stare at her. "Can't you give me one more—"

"Security!" she barks into her walkie-talkie. She glares at you. "I run a safe set. People who don't follow orders get people hurt. You're never going to work in this field. I'll make sure of it."

Great. You're first day as a movie stunt driver is also your last.

For weeks you try to find a job, with no success. Finally you find something that matches your skills. You're a fast-food delivery person.

At least you get to ride every day. . . .

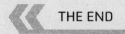

THE END

"A lab," you murmur. You gaze around a room frozen in time. A jacket slung casually over a sofa. An open soda can. You move deeper into the room and pick up a framed photo from the desk: you and your dad at a baseball game. This must be your father's secret lab.

You put the photo back on the desk and notice a large map on the wall. THE GRID is written across the top. "The Grid," you murmur. That's what your dad called the world inside the server he created.

You take a seat at the desk and wipe off the thick dust. This reveals multicolored glowing graphics. The desk itself is a tabletop computer!

You tap the ON button and the screen fills with code. Suddenly, all the gobbledygook on the screen rewrites itself into a very simple question:

TRON PROJECT—"INITIATE SEQUENCE?" Y/N?

Good question.

If you hit Yes, TURN TO PAGE 57.

If you hit No, TURN TO PAGE 12.

If you do nothing, TURN TO PAGE 48.

Quorra speeds toward an enormous mountain. You clench your teeth as she aims straight for it, and you release your white-knuckled grip on your armrests as a hidden door slides open. She drives inside.

You blink, trying to adjust your eyes to the dark tunnel. You're not sure if she's navigating by memory or if the car is doing it for her. Either way, you come safely to a stop soon enough.

Quorra guides you to a platform which rises up into a large dark room. The far wall is made almost entirely of glass. You step out and pause on the threshold, trying to take it all in.

You may have arrived inside a mountain, but the elevator brought you up to one of its dramatic ledges. A vast landscape spreads out before you. The city twinkles in the distance, occasionally flashing with light surges. You can almost feel its energy pulsing. But this tranquil room has the feeling of a sanctuary.

As your eyes adjust to the low light you realize a man is sitting on the floor meditating. You can't believe what you're seeing: a translucent stream of data and equations seems to be coursing through him!

"We have a guest," Quorra announces.

The man slowly rises from the floor and turns around. As he does, the floor around him illuminates and you can see his face.

You gasp.

TURN TO PAGE 100

Soon Quorra calls you to dinner, and you sit down to a feast. You stick to safe topics. You comment on the vintage Light Cycle your dad has parked in the corner of the room. It seems to be displayed as a work of art, not something that gets much use. After more small talk Flynn finally looks you in the eye.

"I guess you have a lot of questions, Sam," he says.

You return his gaze just as directly. "Actually just one."

Your father takes a deep breath. "Why I never came home." He pushes up from the table and crosses to a fireplace. "Those nights when I went to the office . . . I'm sure you've figured out by now I was coming here. I had discovered a way to bring a human form into digital space. And a portal that would allow me to get back out."

"Amazing," you say.

"Yeah . . . it really was," your father says, a dreamy look on his face. "Time works differently here," he continues, focusing again. "You'd think I had been gone an hour when weeks would pass here." He pokes at the burning logs. "But I couldn't stay here all the time. I needed helpers."

"Tron," you say. "And Clu."

He turns and smiles at you. "You remember all those bedtime stories."

"I thought you were just making it all up," you tell him. "But you were really telling me about your days at 'the office.'"

"Exactly."

TURN TO PAGE 55

You manage to yank the disc from your suit and fling it at your opponent.

He somersaults over the arcing disc, then slams his disc to the ground. It drives into the panel underneath you, shattering the spot you stand on.

"*Yah*!" you cry as you drop down and frantically clutch the edges of the hole. You dangle for a moment. "Fine. If that's how you want to play . . ."

You pull yourself back up onto the game platform and instantly roll to avoid another whirring disc.

Your combatant sprints toward you, and you steal a move from his playbook. You hurl your disc at *his* feet. The panels under him shatter and he plunges down, down, down, screaming all the way.

You stay crouched, shaken by the terrible toll of victory. Slowly you rise, glad that at least it's over. That's when you see a platform heading your way. It carries the victor of another match and quickly attaches to your platform.

You groan. These are elimination rounds! Each winner of these first matches has to fight the other winners.

"Wait!" you cry. "Time! Can I get a time-out?"

Unfortunately, you knew the answer before you even asked the question. A big, fat no.

TURN TO PAGE 20

The room pulsates with sound and light. You're mesmerized by the hundreds of people—programs—gyrating to the vibe of the DJs. Every type imaginable is crowded onto the dance floor: beautiful women, thugs, slackers.

You stiffen as Gem leads you past a cluster of booths where sentries sip energy drinks and flirt with the pretty girls sitting among them.

"Relax," Gem says. "They're too busy to notice you."

She brings you to a heavily guarded booth. You hear a high-pitched cackle from a man wearing a silvery white suit. His hair is a similar silvery blond color. In one hand he brandishes a translucent cane.

"That's Castor," Gem says, nodding toward the guy. "If you want to speak to Zuse, you have to go through him."

You and Gem approach the booth.

"Have a sense of humor, Bartik," Castor says to the tough-looking program sitting with him.

"I didn't come here for entertainment," Bartik growls. "It's time. We can all feel it. The boy is on the Grid. He's spurred hope."

Your ears prick up. Is he talking about *you*?

Castor lets out a bored sigh. "And you wish me to ask Zuse to rally the troops. Stir the masses. Am I right?"

TURN TO PAGE 34

You have no choice—it's kill or be killed. You pull out your disc and face the Light Cycle barreling down at you. At least Clu is wearing his visor. It would be too weird to fling a lethal weapon at a guy with your father's face.

Suddenly a new vehicle vaults off a ramp from below and thunders onto the Grid. It looks like a souped-up dune buggy. It swerves ahead of Clu, leaving a fat ribbon of light in its wake. It whips around you, building a light-wall shield. Is it trapping you or saving you?

Clu can't change direction in time and slams into the wall!

He flies off his bike and flips right over you, slamming onto the hard glassy tarmac. The spectators gasp, and you hold your breath.

No, he doesn't derezz. The fight will continue.

The vehicle skids to a halt beside you and the canopy flips open, revealing a masked driver.

"Get in," the driver growls.

The crowd surrounding you is stomping and screaming. They can't wait to watch you battle Clu in hand-to-hand combat. But who is this driver? And what will happen if you get into that souped-up vehicle?

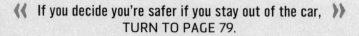

If you decide you're safer if you stay out of the car,
TURN TO PAGE 79.

If you decide to take your chances with the masked driver,
TURN TO PAGE 18.

"This will be our first user since our liberation!" Jarvis continues.

Liberation? What's he talking about?

"Better still, this user also happens to go by the name of Flynn!"

Now the programs all start to boo. Somehow this has to do with your father. You wish you could connect it all together. You have a feeling your life may depend on it.

"So, what to do? What does this user deserve? Might I suggest, perhaps, the challenge of the Grid?"

Now the audience stomps along with the cheers and claps.

"On this very special occasion, who best to battle this singular opponent? Perhaps one who has some experience in these matters."

You thought the crowd couldn't get any louder; you're wrong. They go wild when Clu emerges from the throne ship.

Jarvis makes a sweeping gesture toward Clu. "Oh, yes, indeed! Your liberator! The one who vanquished the tyranny of the user those many cycles before—Clu!"

Clu smirks at you. "So sorry about your dad, kiddo."

Your mind reels. From what they're saying it seems as if Clu and this whole crowd thought of your dad as some kind of oppressor. And that he was destroyed. This doesn't look good.

TURN TO PAGE 113

Better to just do what Jax wants. No point in getting her mad at you on your very first day.

You spend the day watching and learning. There's a lot more to this stunt work than you imagined. No wonder you have to pay your dues and work your way up. Sometimes what you do is beyond boring, but it's still exciting to be around the crew, to watch the scenes and be amazed by the stunts.

On the last day of the film shoot Jax approaches you while you're packing up some gear. "Here, kid," she says, handing you a cup of coffee. "You did good. So I thought I'd be your gopher for a change."

You grin and take the coffee. "Thanks."

"Listen, I just got a call to be the coordinator on a huge new film," Jax says. "I want you to be one of the riders. Maybe use those martial arts I've seen you doing during downtime."

"Really! That's awesome! Thanks."

Jax smiles at you. "You earned it."

This is just the beginning. You move up from stunt man to action star. In fact, after only a few years, you become so successful you buy back Encom and put Alan Bradley in charge. But first he has to promise you that the building can be used in any movie you want.

After all, you've had a lot of practice pulling stunts on that skyscraper!

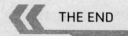

THE END

You and Quorra plow through the chaos.

"Sam, look out!" you hear her shout. She shoves you out of the way and takes a blow to the arm. She crumples to the floor.

At the same moment, the lights short out! The room plunges into inky blackness, punctured by strobing lights.

You can see that the Black Guardsmen are momentarily disoriented, and you use this distraction to gather Quorra up in your arms. You haul her toward the elevator that will bring you back down to the ground. That's when you notice programs around you staring at the elevator in awe.

Your dad. He's standing right outside the elevator! He left the safe house!

And he's the one who shorted out the lights.

"Stay close," he orders, pushing you into the elevator.

Just as the doors are closing, one of the guards fires a grappling hook into the elevator. It attaches to your dad's back and yanks off his disc.

"Your disc!" Quorra murmurs, half-conscious.

TURN TO PAGE 107

You're not sure if you want to mess with this complex computer system right now. You walk away and go back upstairs to check out some of the games you've played before.

You stroll through the arcade's rows. Somehow your desire to play anything is evaporating. The cobwebs, the boarded windows, the general feeling of desolation is getting to you. You're never going to figure out who sent that page. You might as well head for home.

You make your way toward the front door. Suddenly, the skin on the back of your neck tingles. You have the weirdest sensation that you're not alone.

You whip around and—*yes!* You catch sight of a shadowy figure ducking under one of the games!

Is that who sent the page? Or did that person follow you in once you got here? The bigger question is: are you in danger?

The person could have a weapon!

Actually, the biggest question is what to do now!

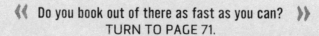

Do you book out of there as fast as you can?
TURN TO PAGE 71.

Or do you confront the intruder ON PAGE 108.

"We have to get out of here—fast!" you say. "Otherwise we'll just be handed over to Clu."

"You're right," your dad says. "But how?"

"With these!" Quorra calls. She waves you over to a storage unit. "Tron Chutes!" She pulls out the bladed wings the Black Guard used when they crashed into the End of Line Club. The three of you quickly slip into the harnesses.

TURN TO PAGE 137

50

You stand, shocked, as a wall in the enormous ship opens. Two figures are illuminated by the lights inside. A ramp descends, and they tromp toward you.

The men wear black skintight suits. Streaks of color flash along the seams of their clothes, as if they were plugged in. The visors on their helmets keep you from being able to see their faces, making them seem sinister. These are the Sentries you've heard about in your dad's bedtime stories. They're the police force of this world.

"This program has no disc," one of them announces. "Another stray."

Huh?

Before you can ask what they mean, they grab you and escort you up into the hovering vehicle.

"Wait!" you protest. They ignore you.

The door slides shut, and the Recognizer lurches upward, flying toward the more brightly lit areas of the city.

TURN TO PAGE 56

You take a peek behind you to try and figure out where everyone is on the Grid.

Who is left on your team? And *are* they your team? You're pretty sure it's you and these candy-colored players against Clu and his Sentries. But that purple program was pretty hostile. Could these guys actually be working against you?

How do you play this game and still stay alive?

Should you work together with the programs or should you try to win this on your own?

You can't trust them to work with you. You're in this alone.
TURN TO PAGE 13.

You're outnumbered without your teammates.
Work together ON PAGE 62.

You gaze out the window. The Portal streams upward from an island as a swirling maelstrom of energy.

"Hang on, everybody!" Quorra cries. "I'm bringing her in!"

Quorra executes a stomach-churning move and lands the vehicle on a rocky shore. You all scramble out, and your dad points up at the Portal. It's flickering faster and faster. "It's getting ready to close!" he shouts over the howling wind.

He leads you and Quorra up a steep stairway carved out of rock. Energy whirls around you. The ground shakes, and you cover your head to keep from being pounded by tumbling rocks. The island is beginning to crumble. You hope you get to the Portal before everything completely falls apart!

You crest the hill and come to a narrow bridge. It stretches out over a void toward the Portal. The bridge is slowly separating! You know you have no choice. You have to cross it—and fast! Only one problem: standing dead center on the bridge between you and the Portal is . . . Rinzler, your dangerous opponent from the Games!

TURN TO PAGE 136

The Sentries stare around, puzzled. That's because you and Quorra are above them, perched in the open crossbeams of the elevator and hidden from view.

You drop down and take them out. Then you dash across the throne room toward the bridge. Two more Sentries rush at you. You and Quorra make quick work of them.

Just then Jarvis, Clu's right-hand man, appears. He looks terrified. Good.

"You can't stop us," you say with a snarl. Quorra holds her disc aloft, ready to throw it.

"Wouldn't dream of it," Jarvis says hastily.

"Keep me covered," you tell Quorra. She nods and crouches, ready to leap to your defense. But Jarvis looks far too frightened and is too much of a wimp to strike back.

You stride to the case and yank out your dad's disc. It feels warm in your hands. You don't have time to gloat, though. More Sentries will arrive any minute.

"What should we do with him?" Quorra asks, jerking her head toward Jarvis.

You look at the sniveling program and shrug. "I have a feeling that once Clu finds out the disc is gone, he'll take care of this guy."

Jarvis sinks to the ground, covering his face and moaning.

TURN TO PAGE 125

You continue into the city. The farther you go, the more apprehensive you become. There's something oppressive about the place—and the few people you see on the streets seem furtive, as if they're hiding from something. Or someone.

Alex must feel it, too. "M-maybe we should go back and check out the stadiums," he says nervously. "We don't have to get to the light."

"We're almost there," you say. "Might as well see what it is."

You arrive at the source of the light—the base of an enormous skyscraper. You walk through the door and realize there's an elevator. You push a button, and up you go.

Alex clutches your arm as the door opens revealing an incredible party in full swing.

People of every description crowd the dance floor. DJs spin thumping beats. Colored lights whirl and flicker, making it hard to see. And beyond the booths, bar, and patrons you can see the amazing skyline through the club's floor-to-ceiling windows.

"I thought we'd find something a lot cooler," Alex complains. "You know, like aliens or spaceships or something."

You try not to laugh. "Hey, we only just got here," you say. "We still could."

"Just a bunch of grown-ups," Alex grumbles. "Boring."

"Give it a chance," you say.

You push him in front of you through the crowd toward the bar. Maybe some juice drink with a fancy straw in it will make him happy.

Then you hear something that stops you dead in your tracks.

TURN TO PAGE 124

Your father turns to gaze out the window.

"We were building a whole new world," he says wistfully. "And then something amazing happened. New beings emerged. I didn't invent them. They just evolved! Real individuals—not simply programs."

"I called them ISOs—Isomorphic algorithm programs," your father goes on.

"So what happened?" you ask.

"Clu happened," your father answers flatly. He faces you, his expression full of pain. "What I saw as a miracle, he saw as a virus in the system. Imperfection. I had programmed him to help create a perfect system, to shut down errors." He shrugs. "Individuality is a threat to such a mind-set."

You start to understand. "Clu thought you'd lost the vision when you welcomed these new kinds of beings. To him they were bad mutations. Computer viruses."

"Exactly," your dad confirms.

"What did he do?" you ask.

He gazes out the window again. "He managed a coup. Nearly killed me. And his next act was the elimination of the new beings—the ISOs."

TURN TO PAGE 87

You're brought to a box-shaped hangar and placed in restraints. People huddle in groups around you, but you're too stunned to attempt speech. Instead, you gaze down through the transparent floor.

You watch the scene below as the Recognizer floats through an enormous cityscape. Spires jut miles up into the blinking blue sky. The scale is huge and makes the gargantuan Recognizer seem tiny by comparison. A pulsing blue energy flickers between the buildings and along the grid—shaped pattern of the city sectors.

"He actually did it," you murmur. You now understand exactly what you are looking at—a fully realized world created by the computer-programming—genius mind of your father.

When you tear your eyes away from the dark, pulsating view, overwhelmed, you notice a young guy staring at you.

"Does the name Kevin Flynn mean anything to you?" you ask the kid.

"Keep quiet if you want to live," he whispers.

Not the reaction you were hoping for . . .

You hear muttering beside you. A sweaty, nervous-looking dude is rubbing his hands over and over. "Not the games, not the games, not the games," he's chanting.

You turn to a man standing on your other side. "What's his problem?" you ask.

He turns to look at you and you stumble backward. Half of his face is gone!

TURN TO PAGE 33

Sure, why not? You hit **Y**.

A blue flash scorches the room, momentarily blinding you. You feel around, trying to shut the machine down. None of the switches do anything.

Finally the little blue dots stop swarming in front of you. You look at the machine. Dead.

"Well, this was useful," you grumble. "Thanks a lot, Alan." You trot back up the stairs and out of the arcade.

A big gust of wind makes the door shut behind you with a loud slam. In the distance you see jagged blue lightning sear the sky. Rain starts to fall, and you shove your hands deeper into your jacket pockets. The area seems even more deserted than when you arrived—if that's possible.

A fog has settled in, obscuring the store windows and signs. Just a blank grayness that feels oppressive. You look forward to sprawling on your sofa with some hot cider and Marv snoozing on your feet, keeping them warm. You arrive at the streetlamp where you locked your bike.

It's gone.

TURN TO PAGE 63

The three of you retreat down the stairs to the middle of the ship. You hide among several large cargo containers.

"What did you see?" you ask your father.

"A Recognizer," he tells you grimly. "And then several more. Like a fleet."

There's a sudden shudder. You and the others brace yourselves against the jerky motions of the solar sailer as it sharply changes course. You peer out a window and see that you're being drawn into an enormous cave. The ship's sails fold back into its body as it prepares to dock.

"What's happening?" you ask.

"A new course," your father says. "This is no longer a nonstop ride to the Portal."

Now what do you do?

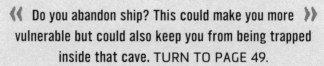

Do you abandon ship? This could make you more vulnerable but could also keep you from being trapped inside that cave. TURN TO PAGE 49.

Or do you stay aboard to find out what's going on? TURN TO PAGE 30.

Clu grips his baton with both hands. He sprints forward and leaps into the air. As he does, the baton transforms into a Light Cycle!

"So that's what this is for!" you cry, waving the baton.

You grin as you hold out the baton, preparing. "Now, *this* I can do!" You run and jump. A Light Cycle forms. You revel in the power surging beneath you.

Then you remember—this is a ride to the death.

You study Clu as the green and blue riders glide onto the humming grid. Your eyes widen. The Light Cycles leave colored walls behind them, like trails.

A cycling Sentry is hot on the tail of the purple rider. It zooms in front of him, then zigzags back and forth, creating a light wall that blocks the purple player. Unable to change course in time, the purple program slams into the wall, derezzing into thousands of tiny cubes.

The light walls are lethal, you realize.

Clu shoots down to the level below and decapitates the blue player with his disc.

Whoa. This guy means business. You have to focus.

Two Sentries sandwich you between them. You surge out toward an off-ramp. It's a high-risk maneuver but one you've done on regular freeways before.

One of the Sentries tries to emulate your move but can't. He derezzes in a churning wipeout on the Grid. "Score!" you cheer.

TURN TO PAGE 51

There are already dozens of solar sailers on the deck of the huge ship.

"Let's get out of here," you say.

"Yeah," your dad agrees. He nods to the crates. "We don't want to be here when they start unloading these guys."

You scurry along the ramp leading to the dock and keep low, hoping you won't be noticed in all the activity.

"This way." Your father leads you quickly along the edges of the deck and up a spiral staircase. You sneak onto a catwalk, high above the deck of the Rectifier. You can see hundreds of programs—maybe thousands—standing below. Then you see Clu approaching a podium. A wave of cheers greets him.

He smiles broadly as he addresses the throng. "Together, we have achieved a great many things. We've built a new world. We've rid it of its imperfections. And we rid it of the false deity who sought to enslave us: Kevin Flynn."

This is so bizarre. There's Clu—an exact replica of your father—a younger version of your father, sure, but still your father. And he's declaring *himself* as the enemy! If this is weird for you, you can only imagine how it must be for your dad. Clu went from being creation to partner to enemy.

TURN TO PAGE 74

Now you understand. That man isn't your father. He's *Clu*, your father's avatar! He's a program!

No wonder he hasn't changed. He looks exactly the way he did when your father created him. Your dad designed Clu to look just like him.

He runs this alternate world. And these life-and-death games.

How do you reason with a computer program?

No time to wonder about that now—the Sentries have returned and drag you out.

"Hey, you don't have to play so rough," you tell them. "I'm going."

The ship lowers so that it hovers just above the sprawling game grid. The gaunt man, Jarvis, descends the ramp onto the Grid, carrying an ornate box.

The Sentries drag you down to the Grid and you gaze up at the thousands of programs. You wonder where Clu is.

Jarvis clears his throat, then addresses the throngs. "Greetings, programs. Oh, what an occasion we have here before us. His Beneficence has given us the pleasure and the privilege of the games for many a cycle!"

You guess that Clu is the "beneficence" Jarvis means. And that Clu invented the gladiator games.

"On this occasion, we will witness something altogether different! The rumors are true. We do, indeed, have a user in our midst!"

The crowd cheers. User? You glance around. Oh! They mean you!

TURN TO PAGE 45

You've got to work together—otherwise there's no chance of survival. If you eliminate Clu's wingmen, you might actually have a shot at surviving.

You zoom toward the kid in aqua. "Follow me!" you shout.

You increase speed to catch up with a Sentry. You and Aqua take positions on either side of him. You move closer, boxing him in. The Sentry bumps Aqua, sending him sprawling off his bike. He slides along the floor.

The Sentries bear down on the helpless kid, unsheathing his disc. You've got to stop him. You go even faster on your Light Cycle. You zip in front of the Sentry, and he slams into your trailing light wall. He derezzes!

Aqua is stunned to be alive. He raises his arms in triumph. The crowd screams with delight at this amazing sight.

Then Clu races over and flattens the kid under his Light Cycle, derezzing him into tiny cubes.

TURN TO PAGE 7

"No!" you shout. "No, No, NO, NO, NO!!!"

You stomp around the streetlamp. You can't believe this! You run out into the intersection hoping you'll catch a glimpse of your bike's taillights. You come to a standstill and blink a few times. "This doesn't look familiar," you murmur.

You know you haven't been to this part of town in a while, but somehow the street seems different from when you arrived just a few minutes ago. Maybe it's because of the fog.

Suddenly a blinding spotlight pierces the gloom, bathing you in bright white light.

You shade your eyes with your hand and squint up into the night sky. Your eyes widen. "Impossible!" you gasp. "Th-that looks like a . . . like a . . ."

Hovering silently above you is a Recognizer—the same upside-down U—shaped vehicle that sits in plastic mini form on your shelf at home. Your old night light—only a gazillion times bigger!

It can't be. But there it is. And there's only one possible explanation.

I . . . I'm inside the computer! you realize. In the system!

Panic rushes through you and you start to run. A loud rumbling sound makes you look down. *No!* The ground around your feet is shrinking! You're left trying to balance on a tiny concrete island, surrounded by a trench. You're not going anywhere.

"Identify yourself, program!" a booming voice orders from the Recognizer.

TURN TO PAGE 50

Moments later, you rev your father's old Light Cycle as you ride toward the city rising in the distance.

At the center of the city is a monolithic skyscraper, sending out a pulsing light show from the very top of its spire. You remember seeing it from the Recognizer.

You cross a long narrow bridge and ride into the tangle of city streets. The energy crackles. This must be the energy Quorra meant—programs and their vehicles can't travel anywhere without it.

You're surrounded by massive buildings with severe angular designs. They tower over you, making you feel tiny and insignificant.

Above you, a Recognizer cruises lazily, but you don't seem to have attracted attention. There are other vehicles and programs that also ignore you. So far, so good.

Soon the scene changes around you. Now the buildings are smaller, more rundown. More Sentries are out on patrol. You hear a booming voice announcing, "This is a restricted area. Authorized programs only. Violators without functionality or residence confirmation will be swiftly deleted."

You see Sentries manning each corner, checking disc IDs of passing programs. You decide you'll attract less attention on foot so you ride into an alley and reluctantly leave your dad's bike there.

TURN TO PAGE 92

You turn around. "What makes you think I'm looking for someone?" you ask.

She steps up to you and smirks. She plucks the card Quorra gave you from your hand. "Intuition," she says drily.

Your eyes narrow as you study her. How much should you reveal?

"I can help you, Sam," she says. "I know who you're looking for. And you'll have better luck with me than on your own."

She has a point. You nod slowly.

"My name is Gem. Come with me." She links her arm though yours. "Whisper into my ear," she tells you.

"Huh?"

"Just do it."

Whatever. You lean into her and whisper, "I suppose you have a reason. . . ."

She laughs as if you're saying something brilliantly funny and waves at the nearby Sentries. They let you pass without a question.

The doors at the entrance slide open, revealing a glass elevator. You step inside and *whoosh*! The elevator rockets up the side of the building to the top.

The elevator stops and the door opens into a teeming nightclub. It overlooks the city. Gem takes your hand and walks you into the crowd.

"What is this place?" you ask.

"It's called the End of Line Club," she tells you.

TURN TO PAGE 43

"Slow down, kiddo," you tell him. "First answer my questions."

The kid rolls his eyes and sighs, as if this is the most boring conversation ever. "My name is Alex, and I've been sneaking in here for years." He gives you a smug smile. "It's not as locked up as you think."

You cock your head. "Years? You've been coming here since you were in diapers? You're not exactly old."

Alex scowls, then his forehead furrows. "Wait a sec! Who are *you*? And what are you doing in here?"

"You ask too many questions," you tell him, suppressing a grin. You turn back to the computer screen. "Now let's see what I can do with this baby."

Alex crosses his arms and pouts as you shove his chair out of the way. You stand, gazing down at the console. "Hmmmm."

Suddenly Alex dashes in front of you. "I know!" he cries. "I bet the screen is interactive. No buttons to push!" His fingers hover over the screen, and then he circles the area called the Outlands. He presses down.

There is a blinding light and then—*whoosh!* You feel as if all the air is being sucked out of you. Crazy lights swirl around your eyes, and your feet fly out from under you. But you don't fall—well, not exactly. It feels more like weightless free fall.

What is going on?

TURN TO PAGE 106

Time to get serious. You shove Zuse off the bar. He goes sprawling into the crowd. They cheer even louder and hoist him up over their heads. Then they ferry him across the front of the bar.

You scan the room and spot Bartik glowering with his gang at Zuse's booth. You cup your hands around your mouth to be heard over the music. "Zuse!" you cry. "I found Zuse!"

That catches Bartik's attention. He shoves his way toward you. You point at the club owner, who is still being passed around by the crowd. "Castor is Zuse!"

Okay, now you've got *everyone's* attention. Zuse thuds to the ground, and space clears around him. Bartik lifts him up by his shoulders.

"You're Zuse?" Bartik bellows. "You . . . cartoon?"

"Desperate times, desperate fashion choices," Zuse quips. Then his eyes narrow and he lowers his voice. "I've had to protect my interests. Lay low. I'm sure you understand. . . ."

Bartik releases Zuse. He turns to the crowd. "The time of revolution is upon us! And if this former leader will no longer lead—then we take on Clu ourselves!" He whirls and glares at Zuse again. "But first we punish this turncoat for making fools of us all!"

Just then, the Black Guard charge down the stairs and start hurling discs.

"About time," Zuse rolls his eyes. "So hard to find good backup anymore."

TURN TO PAGE 84

A small door opens, flooding the chamber with bright white light. It's the only exit. You step though it and find yourself and another person on a floating platform in an arena filled with hundreds of thousands of spectators. Seven other large courts float in the middle of the massive stadium, allowing spectators to watch multiple matches at once.

A deafening roar builds as the platform you're on whirls and locks into place. If only you could figure out exactly what you'll be playing . . .

Silence settles over the arena. You've never seen anything on this kind of scale before. All attention seems to be riveted on a ship hovering above the stadium. You peer up and see an imposing masked man dressed in militaristic armor displayed on a large screen. He brings his arm down sharply, and the crowd erupts. The games have begun.

Your combatant faces you and pulls his disc from the sheath in the back of his suit. A visor extends from his helmet, shielding his face. He brandishes the disc and you notice its laser-sharp edges. You realize you've seen him before!

"I have a three-inch version of you on my shelf," you joke.

The combatant hurls his disc at your head. You duck, but it clips your hair, singeing it! The disc returns to his hand like a boomerang.

"But he never did that!" you blurt out.

TURN TO PAGE 36

You stare out at the Sea of Simulation. It's not really water, you remind yourself as intense colors tumble like waves. You bend down and waggle your hand in the flickering energy ebbing and flowing around your feet. You feel a slight tremor, not as bad as getting a shock—more like mild static electricity. You can handle this.

You wade into the energy. It tingles but it's not unpleasant. It sort of tickles, in fact.

The Recognizer is moving very slowly along the coast, so you have no trouble keeping up with it. You follow the ship for quite some time, wondering why it hasn't noticed you. But something weird is happening—more and more twirling energy bursts are appearing around you. Some are beginning to attach themselves to you. Your thoughts grow more and more confused. It's harder to think now. You can barely see the Recognizer. That's when you realize you are under the sea.

You peer through the murky churning energy field in front of you. Images appear and recede—ghostly shapes and figures. You reach toward one and realize your arm is changing right in front of you. Your edges are growing blurry; your fingers elongate, then snap back into place. Your whole body seems to be having some kind of molecular breakdown!

The energy of the Sea of Simulation is transforming your body into something else—something strange and unfamiliar. Soon you've lost all sense of who you are or why you're there. You simply allow the energy to take you. Swallow you up. Mutate you into something no longer human—and since you're no longer human, you don't actually mind.

THE END

70

Now the kid looks intrigued. "Not even you?"

You smirk. "I own the place. I can be here as much as I want."

He looks around skeptically at the grimy surfaces, the cobwebs, and the boarded-up windows. "I guess you don't want to be here too much."

"That's the truth," you tell him. "Come on, let's get out of here. Nothing but ghosts and dust bunnies." You lead him out the door. Just as you thought—this whole night has just been a silly wild-goose chase.

"Hey, if a ghost got into a fight with a dust bunny, who do you think would win?" the kid asks. "And if it was the ghost of a dust bunny do you think it would hop? And—"

This kid is beginning to give you a headache. You'll be glad to be rid of him. Just the way you'll be glad to be rid of this arcade. You take one glance back over your shoulder and vow never to step foot in it again.

THE END

You're not sticking around to find out who is in the arcade with you. This place is creepy enough! You tear out of the arcade and into the deserted streets, your heart thumping.

You slow down as you approach your motorcycle, starting to feel foolish. Running out of there like a scared little kid, as if you were being chased by a monster or something.

There is probably nothing to be scared of. Nothing.

You whirl around and return to the arcade, determined to figure out who the intruder is. You poke your head in cautiously. No one in sight.

You creep into the building and drop down, scanning under the game machines. Still nothing. You stand back up, confused. You're pretty sure no one followed you out to the street. So where did the intruder go?

You stay close to the wall as you make your way along the perimeter of the arcade. You don't want anyone to catch you by surprise.

Still nothing. No sign of life.

Then you hear a loud *whoop!* from downstairs, followed by something that sounds like an explosion!

And it came from your dad's private lab!

TURN TO PAGE 25

"I am not a program!" you declare.

A new voice comes over the speaker. "Identify yourself," it rumbles.

You're startled. There's something familiar about the voice. How can that be possible? You don't know anyone in this crazy world. Still, you answer truthfully: "My name is Sam Flynn!"

Your declaration echoes around the hushed stadium. For a moment there's total silence. Then a murmur starts in the crowd. They seem to recognize the name.

Good. Your dad invented this whole world—maybe now they'll show you some respect!

Your opponent approaches you, flanked by two Sentries. They escort you off the platform and up onto the ship without saying a word. "Not very chatty, are you?" you say. No response. At least you're not fighting for your life anymore. You hope.

They bring you into what that looks like a regal throne room. A figure wearing a cloak stands with his back to you, gazing down onto the courts. A thin man with gaunt features stands beside him, studying you. The Sentries leave, and the man in the cloak turns to face you. He's wearing a helmet.

"Who are you?" you ask as he slowly circles you.

The man stops and removes his helmet.

You gasp. "Dad!"

TURN TO PAGE 22

Time to end this party! You slip out your disc and hurl it at the booming speakers. There's a *fzzzzt* sound, and sparks fly as they short out.

The only sound now is the DJ, who is still humming whatever was just playing. Apparently his headphones are still working, and the song continues running on his deck.

"This program wants to put an end to your fun!" Zuse declares. "He hates dancing! Music! Good times."

You groan. What is he getting at?

"This man is—" you declare loudly, grabbing Zuse's arm.

"The party king!" someone in the crowd shouts.

"Quit killing our good times!"

"That's just what he wants to do!" Zuse shouts. "He is bent on destroying all pleasures! This is just the beginning of his oppression!"

The crowd's growing ugly. The low murmur has turned into a rumble. They advance on you, pulling out their discs.

"No! No! He's got it wrong!" you protest. "I'm not the one who—"

But it's no use. They attack!

"Too bad. You had such promise as a competitive dancer," Zuse says, just before you black out. Forever.

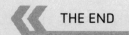

THE END

"We've been kept in the dark too long," Clu continues. "All that we've known is not all there is. Fellow programs, our world is a cage no more. The key to the next frontier is finally in our possession."

He gestures up at the bridge and all eyes follow, yours included. Your eyes grow wide. There's your father's disc, glowing inside an elaborate case. Cheers erupt from the crowd.

Quorra clutches your arm. "He's going to use Flynn's disc to travel through the Portal!"

"He's getting out," you say, "and bringing an army with him!"

"He's surpassed me," your father murmurs. Then he gives his head a sharp shake. "We have to stop him."

"Are you ready to receive your command?" Clu thunders below. "Out there is our destiny!"

He brings one arm down in a dramatic gesture. Several banners drop to the floor, revealing mocked up images of Rectifiers hovering over major cities of the United States. The images shift to show the same pictures over Europe and Asia. Then they pull back to display Rectifiers surrounding Earth itself.

The one unchanging image is of the glowing blue portal. The way out of this world—and into yours.

TURN TO PAGE 117

"Okay, Dad," you murmur, focusing on the mission. "Come out, come out, wherever you are."

You're not really sure where to begin. The Outlands are vast, and you're trying to find a single person. Needle, meet haystack.

Bartik and Veltor thought your dad might have retreated into the mountains in case Clu eventually invented vehicles that could go off-grid. You head that way.

You trudge across the dark and desolate landscape. The terrain is rugged, and you're glad you stay in shape with all of your activities. Though as you get closer to the foot of a towering, jagged mountain range, you really wish you'd brought some mountain-climbing gear.

This is crazy, you think. How am I ever going to find him? And even if I do, it may be too late. Whatever Clu has in mind, it could already be happening. Bartik and Veltor both stressed that time is short.

Still, they felt strongly that without your father, there's no way to rally enough support to overthrow Clu. An idea occurs to you. Could being the son of Kevin Flynn be good enough?

You wish you could ask Bartik and Veltor what they think. *Man, why hasn't anyone here invented cell phones*? But they don't exist. The decision is yours alone.

If you continue searching for your father,
TURN TO PAGE 115.

If you return to the city,
TURN TO PAGE 102.

"I'll give you one more chance to hand over your disc," the Sentry orders.

"What do you want my disc for?" you ask. "Don't you have one of your—*whoa*!"

Before you can complete your sentence he flings his disc. You duck and it returns to his hand. He speaks into a device on his wrist. "Rogue program. Derezz in process."

"I don't think so," you taunt. "I'm not like other guys. I don't derezz so easy."

He flicks the disc at you again, and this time you execute a high leap and kick him in the face. You spin around as he's recovering and race away.

You hurtle around the corner and run smack into another Sentry.

"Present your disc," the Sentry orders.

You jerk your thumb behind you. "That guy took it! I've been robbed!"

"Describe your assailant," the Sentry demands.

Oops. "Sorry! Dark. Didn't get a good look! Traumatized! You know." You start running again.

"That's the rogue program!" you hear the first Sentry shout.

Two discs suddenly slice into you—one into your arm, the other into your leg. You drop to the ground, pain burning through you.

They hover over you. One of them raises his disc. Then it comes down, and there is nothing but . . . darkness.

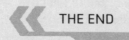

THE END

You stare openmouthed up at the ship. It seems familiar, but how is that possible? Then it hits you—it's a giant-size version of your old night light. A vehicle your dad called a Recognizer!

You can't ignore the truth anymore. The map, the city, the sea. You have known all along. You're *inside* the world your dad invented. Could this be where your dad went all those years ago? Could he still be here?

You can't think about that right now. You have to figure out some way to get Alex back.

The Recognizer is moving slowly out over the Sea of Simulation. It must be cruising around looking to snatch up programs. You wonder why it didn't grab you—unless it was because you weren't as close to the sea as Alex. Perhaps you need to get closer.

TURN TO PAGE 69

78

Silence. Darkness.
Nothingness. Until . . .

You float, your mind a blank, through a stream of luminescent data.

Then . . . you're back at the arcade, your head down on the computer console. You sit up and blink. Was it all some kind of crazy dream?

"Whatcha doing, kid?" you hear a voice behind you. "Knocking on the sky . . . ?"

You turn and gaze at your dad. He's standing in the middle of the room with Quorra. She has a completely amazed look on her face.

"Yeah," you say, getting up. "And listening to the sound."

You can't stop the grin from spreading across your face. "We should get out of here," you say. "This lady's never seen a sunset."

You go upstairs to the arcade floor, the others close behind. "I should reopen this place," your dad says. "I kinda like these old-school games."

"Yeah," you agree with a laugh. "It's hard to imagine a pinball machine trying to take over the world!"

Together, the three of you walk out . . . into a brand-new day.

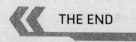

THE END

No way do you trust a maniac driver in a mask! "Not a chance!" you shout and turn to run.

You hear the vehicle *vroom* after you. And Clu now heads straight toward you. They're boxing you in! Was that their plan all along?

"Get in!" you hear behind you. "Now!"

Clu is barreling down on you. At the very last moment you fling yourself to the side—and Clu smashes right into the car that's chasing you!

The crowd goes crazy. You use the distraction to do a somersault off the platform to the game grid below. Then the platform below that. You don't care where you're going—you just go!

You're panting hard when you finally find a way out of the stadium. You stop to get your bearings. Up ahead you see a bridge that leads into a city. All around you are other stadiums. Kind of what you imagine an Olympic village to be like. Neither option seems very safe. But you know you can't stay here. The Sentries are probably already looking for you.

Take the bridge into the city ON PAGE 120.

Seek shelter in one of the nearby stadiums ON PAGE 19.

You fling yourself at Rinzler. He parries your tackle and judo flips you. You slam onto the bridge, the air knocked out of you.

As you struggle to your feet you see Quorra leap into action. She pulls out her baton, and a grappling hook shoots out. She uses it to swing herself under the swaying bridge past your dad and Rinzler. She flips up beside you and helps you to your feet.

Rinzler draws his discs and stalks toward you and Quorra.

You feel an enormous shudder and are horrified to see that the bridge is retracting from each end! A gap is widening in the center of the bridge.

"What's happening?" you shout over the roaring winds.

"The bridge does this when the Portal is about to close," your father shouts back. He's staggering toward the ever-widening gap. Rinzler still stands between you. You clutch the bridge rail to keep from being tipped over into the infinite chasm below.

Rinzler whirls around to face your father again. "You're never getting out, Flynn," he snarls.

You've got to do something. The Portal will close any minute, and you'll all be trapped here! But what?

Do you use your disc to try to derezz Rinzler? Your aim has to be perfect or you could hit your dad. TURN TO PAGE 97.

Do you use Quorra's grappling hook and try to bypass Rinzler, grab your dad, and get back before the Portal closes? Complicated, but it could work. TURN TO PAGE 89.

Trying to escape sounds like a really good way to get killed. And you are pretty sure you don't want this guy bossing you around. You carefully extract yourself from the huge guy's grip. "Sorry. I'm not much of a joiner."

The mountain of a man steps back and glares at you. "You will regret that."

Now you get nervous. You're trapped in a small cell with a guy who takes up most of the space in it.

"You know, on second thought—"

You never get to finish your sentence. The man's enormous pawlike hand suddenly grips your throat. "You know too much," he hisses into your ear as he lifts you off the ground. "And now we could never trust you. You must be eliminated."

You struggle, wriggling and kicking, but it's no use. The giant is just too strong. The world spins, and then everything goes black.

THE END

You've got to take out Rinzler or the Portal will close and trap you all here forever.

"Look out, Dad!" you shout. You grab your disc and hurl it at Rinzler's head. He smacks it with his baton, and it careens back at you. You lurch to the side to avoid being sliced by the whirling disc.

Unfortunately, your dad and Quorra both lunge the same way, and the sudden weight of all three of you tilts the already precarious bridge. All of you topple over the side . . . and into the yawning chasm below. This is your . . .

END.

You are whisked away to a sparse chamber, where you are outfitted by a group of four beautiful and identical Sirens. You're impressed by the form-fitting armor they give you, but you are worried. Why would you need to wear armor? You shudder, remembering that the nervous dude would rather fling himself to his death than play.

One of the Sirens removes a luminescent disc from a container and stands behind you. She inserts it into a sheath in your armor. The disc hums and glows. "Mirroring complete," the Siren states. "Disc activated and synchronized."

"What is that?" you ask.

The Sirens look confused by the question.

"I'm new to this whole"—you gesture broadly—"this whole scene."

"The disc holds all of your information. It is who you are," one of the Sirens says. "We all have them."

"He is different," another Siren states.

"You're ready," a third Siren declares. "Proceed to games."

"Games? What am I supposed to do?" you ask.

"Survive," the fourth Siren says. You stare, open-mouthed, as they melt into the walls and freeze into statues.

"S-survive?" you stammer. What kinds of games *are* these?

TURN TO PAGE 68

Zuse leaps up onto the bar and starts dancing across it, like an old-fashioned vaudeville performer doing a soft-shoe number. A spotlight shoots out of his cane, marking your every move.

"Behold the Son of Flynn!" he cries. "Behold the son of our maker!"

All the guards are now focused on you. Another disc spins across the room right at your head when—

Clack! A disc flies in from the opposite direction, deflecting the weapon away from you. You spin around and see Quorra striding through the club!

You race to her, ducking through the crowd, trying to put programs between you and the Black Guard. Maybe they won't be able to aim as effectively with so many distractions and obstacles.

Quorra does a double take when she sees Zuse dancing on the bar. The disappointment on her face is obvious.

"Come on," you urge her. You know seeing her old mentor Zuse acting like a cartoon is unsettling, but now is not the time.

TURN TO PAGE 47

"Third call for winks on the upper level," the new guy shouts at you. "Move it. Or it will be your hide!"

You'd better get on this winks problem. Even if you have no idea what the problem is! All you can figure is that "winks" are seriously important here.

You find a box labeled WINKS. You don't even bother to check inside. You just grab it and rush upstairs. You come to a sudden stop at the edge of the game platform.

You're at a tiddledywinks tournament and in charge of keeping the winks flowing. Who knew something *this* boring was part of your dad's cool digital world!

The tournament may not *really* last forever—but it sure feels that way!

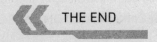

THE END

From where you're standing you don't see any way back to your world. The stretch of land you're on is desolate and almost desertlike. You have a feeling you're not going to be able to get back home unless you find the missing arcade. At least, that's your theory. For all you know, there could be exits and entrances all over the place.

"Come on!" Alex says, grabbing your arm and tugging hard. "What are you waiting for?"

He's right. And then it hits you. Something amazing has just happened: you somehow ended up *inside* a world created by your father. You'll worry about getting back home later. You rack your brain, trying to remember the map on your dad's office wall and on the console. Alex pushed on the Outlands—so that must be where you are now. Then that should be the main city, you reason, looking to your left. And those lights are coming from the Sea of Simulation. Whatever that is.

So which way do you go?

Do you head for the glittering city ON PAGE 119.

Or do you check out those amazing bursts of light at the Sea of Simulation ON PAGE 37.

Your father's face is full of sadness. "I *tried* to come home. But the way out—the Portal—closed on me." He takes in your confused expression. "As a fail-safe I'd set the door to open only from the outside and only for a limited time. It closed on me. That was the last night I ever saw you."

"You mean I can't just go back out the way I came in?" you ask nervously.

"'Fraid not," your dad says.

"The Portal," you press. "It activated when I came in, right? So it's open now."

"For a time, yes." Your father nods. "Not for long."

"So what are we waiting for?" you declare, standing up. "Let's get out of here!"

"The moment Flynn's on the Grid," Quorra says, speaking up for the first time, "Clu will stop at nothing to obtain his disc."

"My disc is everything," your dad explains.

"So that's it? We do nothing? We just sit here?"

"It's amazing how productive doing nothing can be," your father says.

TURN TO PAGE 96

"I'm not sitting around here until some plan magically presents itself," you tell Quorra. "If he refuses to save himself, then I will save myself."

"How?" she asks.

"I'm going through the Portal. Clu wants my dad's disc—not mine. Clu had it and handed it right back. I'm getting out. I'll find Alan, and we're going to figure this thing out from the other side. It may be Clu's game here, but in my world, he's gone in one keystroke."

You seem to have gotten Quorra's attention. She studies you intently.

"I can't do anything until I'm out," you continue. "And I can't get out unless someone gets me to the Portal."

You watch her. Will she help you?

Her expression is unreadable. "I really think you should consider your father's wisdom," she says. She turns and leaves.

Looks like you're on your own. You're going to get out of here, or die trying.

You just hope it's not the second thing. . . .

TURN TO PAGE 135

It's a crazy move, but it's all you've got. You grab Quorra's grappling hook, attach it to the rail the way she did, and swing under the bridge. You rise up through the gap.

"Dad!" you shout at the height of your swing. "Jump!"

He leaps at you and grabs the rope just above your head. His knees hit you in the face, but his added weight actually helps swing you back to the other side fast.

Too bad Rinzler is still on your side of the gap!

"Get us out of here, Dad!" you cry. "We'll hold him off!"

Quorra quickly converts her grappling hook into a weapon.

"I won't be needing this anymore!" You fling your disc at Rinzler. As Rinzler ducks out of the way, your father cries, "Ready!"

You rush to stand beside him and Quorra. Quorra holds her baton in front of her like a spear, holding Rinzler at bay. "Don't let him have any contact," your dad cries. The island is rumbling and shattering around you!

Your dad throws his disc to the pulsating ground, then grabs you and Quorra by the shoulders. "On my count!" he tells Quorra. She keeps jabbing at Rinzler, who struggles inch-by-inch toward you as more and more chasms open up around him.

"Now!" your father cries. He brings his foot down onto his disc, shattering it into pieces. At the same moment, Quorra shoves her baton at Rinzler one last time and releases it. There's a massive wave of energy, you hear an enormous blast, and bright white lights nearly blind you.

TURN TO PAGE 78

"Sorry, man," you say. "Didn't mean to crowd you. Just trying to keep the kid from being trampled." Bartik eyes you suspiciously, but his grip loosens a little. "Small fry are easy to trip over. Always underfoot. Am I right?"

Now he looks completely confused. "Kid? Small fry? What are you talking about?"

"Me, you big loser!" Alex declares. Then he punches your arm. "I hate being called small fry. I'm not *that* small for my age."

"Sorry, sorry," you tell Alex, grateful that his presence is such a distraction to Bartik and his fierce buddies. "Didn't mean to insult you."

Now they're ignoring you and staring wide-eyed at Alex. They almost seem frightened by him. What gives?

Alex scowls at them. "Take a picture, it will last longer," he says. He tugs your sleeve. "Can we go now? Please?"

You're torn. These men know something about your father. Could he actually be alive? And here—in this world? If you walk away now you may never find out.

But they are seriously scary dudes, and their bizarre, fearful response to an eight-year-old kid with braces makes you want to get away from them—fast. Who knows what they do when they feel threatened? Animals usually attack—maybe that's also true for these guys.

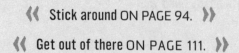

Stick around ON PAGE 94.

Get out of there ON PAGE 111.

You glance at Quorra, who eyes you over her tea. "Aren't you tired of living in hiding?" you ask her. "Fearing for your life? If you can even call this a life."

"It's not for me to interfere," she says, getting up. "This is for the Flynns to decide." She leaves the room.

"It's unfair to project your burdens onto others," your father says. "Stress is bad for the system."

"Giving up is bad for the system!" you shout. "Being a prisoner is bad for the system! Why don't you get it?"

Your father slowly stands and studies you. He seems to be making a decision. "You're right. We're individuals who need to be allowed to make our own choices—and our own mistakes. My way isn't necessarily your way."

He goes to the window and points at a blinking tower. "That's the Portal. As long as it sends out beams it's open. See how it's flickering? That means it's getting ready to close. To be honest, I doubt you'll reach it in time—if you reach it at all. But that's your risk to take. If you want to attempt it, I'll provide you with a map and the means."

He turns and gazes at you. "But I'm staying here. I can't take the chance Clu will get my disc."

So what do you do?

Leave your dad and hope the Portal will still be open by the time you get there? TURN TO PAGE 112.

Or figure he's right and you won't be able to get out—and stay here with him and Quorra where it's safe. TURN TO PAGE 132.

You peer out of the alley. Looks like the Sentries are busy hassling someone else right now. You creep out and hurry to the gigantic tower rising high into the sky.

You reach the base and realize the symbol on the card Quorra gave you is also on the door of the massive structure. This must be the right place.

"Sam Flynn," you hear a female voice say.

You turn and see one of the Sirens who had helped you into your suit of armor back at the games.

You're not sure if you can trust anyone—particularly someone who knows your name, now that you are aware of what's going on between your dad and Clu.

You turn and start to walk away.

"You're looking for someone," she calls after you.

If you keep walking, TURN TO PAGE 23.

If you turn back around, TURN TO PAGE 65.

Castor leads you to the center of the room and somehow activates a staircase that emerges from the floor.

This place is full of bells and whistles, you think, following Castor up the stairs.

You step into a room made entirely of glass. Castor's sanctuary is built under a huge skylight and has a glass floor, so that he can watch what's happening in his club, you suppose.

"You've caused quite the stir with your arrival," Castor tells you. "Whispers of revolution are gaining volume." He turns and pours some drinks.

"So when do I meet Zuse?" you ask.

He turns around, drinks in hand. "You just did." He grins.

You stare at him. "*You're* Zuse? You're not exactly what I pictured."

He shrugs. "After the purge I needed to reinvent myself. Self-preservation, you understand." He hands you your drink. "I've been around since the earliest days of the gaming grid. I have survived by minding all the angles." He takes a sip of his drink. "Now what can I do for you?"

"I need to get to the Portal," you say.

He looks out to the tall structure in the distance. "It's quite the journey. Beyond the far reaches of the Outlands and over the Sea of Simulation."

"So, can you help me?"

TURN TO PAGE 21

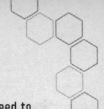

"Don't worry, Alex," you say. "We'll go soon. I just need to have some grown-up talk with these gentlemen first."

"Is it a mini?" Bartik asks, pointing at Alex.

"Are you guys freaks or something? Don't call me *it*!" Alex fumes.

You're confused by their reaction. Then it hits you. You're inside your father's digital world. These are computer-generated programs!

"*It* is a child," you explain. "I used to be one. And Kevin Flynn was one, too. And there's a reason we have this in common. We're very close. Like family. In fact, we *are* family." You take a step back to see what affect your words have.

Exactly what you'd hoped. Their suspicious looks transform into awe. "You are the Son of Flynn," Bartik whispers hoarsely. "You're why the Portal is lit once again."

"I don't know about any Portal," you say. "But yes, Kevin Flynn is my dad. And it sounds to me like you know something about what's happened to him."

Bartik glances at Veltor, who gives a sharp nod.

"Headquarters. It will be safer to talk there."

TURN TO PAGE 105

If that person who streaked through is being chased, you want to find out by whom—or what.

You cross the room and peer through the doorway to the left. This is another enormous dark room. Off in the corner you see the shadowy outlines of a figure, but it's not very distinct.

That's weird, you think, rubbing your eyes. It's as if I can't focus my eyes.

You move deeper into the room and hear strange rustling sounds. Rats, maybe? Then you feel something brush your face. "Hey!" you yelp. You whirl around. But no one's there.

The figure is on the move again. It's almost as if it's leading you somewhere. You round a corner and see it drop through a trapdoor. Now voices are urging you to *follow . . . follow . . . follow.*

What is going on? You whip your head around again, trying to figure out who's talking to you. Your eyes widen—hundreds of ghostly figures are reaching out to you.

"*Yaaaaa*!" you cry, and fall backward through the trapdoor. You land, hard—breaking your neck.

You have fallen victim to the ghost programs—programs that have been deleted but exist in shadowy form at the edges of the Grid.

While they may unfortunately be ghost programs, you're now a full-fledged ghost.

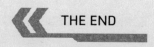

THE END

You look back and forth between your dad and Quorra. "That doesn't make any sense! We have to make a run for it."

"We're safe here in the Outlands," your dad says. "As soon as we step on that Grid—believe me—there's no move we can make Clu hasn't considered. Nothing happens unless he wants it to."

"That's not true," you protest. "Look at me. I'm here. We're together."

Now your dad and Quorra exchange a cryptic look.

"Tell me," your dad says, "what brought you here to the Grid?"

"Alan got a page from you," you say impatiently. Your dad knows all this!

"I didn't send any page, Sam," your dad says.

Your jaw drops. Is he saying what you think he's saying?

"It was Clu," you father says, confirming your fear. "*That's* why you're here. He wanted a new piece on the board to change the game. And with you he got more than he ever dreamed. This is precisely what he wants. Us together. Heading for the Portal. It's his game now, Sam. And the only way to win is not to play."

"That's a stupid way to live," you snap.

"Perhaps," your father says.

"We can go *home*," you argue, almost pleading. "Don't you want that?'"

"Sometimes life has a way of moving you past things like wants and hopes. Quorra will show you to your room. Good night, Sam."

TURN TO PAGE 133

You don't have time to waste. You fling your disc at Rinzler. In the gladiator games you learned how to put the right spin on it to get it to return to you. You keep throwing it—faster and faster. You can see that Rinzler is getting rattled as he ducks and weaves. The bridge undulates and shakes, making it hard for him to keep his balance.

Finally Rinzler manages to throw his discs at you. You take aim and—*clack*! Your disc hits one, then the other, and sends them both over the bridge.

"No!" he shouts. As he reaches out to try and grab them, he loses his balance and tumbles over the side. You hear him scream all the way down.

There is no time to waste. Your father leaps across the gap in the bridge and you all rush to the Portal. But Quorra takes a step backward.

"I'm not going," she says. "This is my world. I want to stay here to ensure we never go through something like this again."

You gaze at her in admiration. "I guess I understand." You grin. "And we'll work on making a safe way in and out so we can visit each other."

Quorra waves good-bye as your father steps up to the Portal.

"Hey, kid," he says. "You owe me a bike."

"Don't worry, Dad," you reply. "There's one with your name on it at my place. And I can't wait for you to meet my dog, Marv. He's a mutt."

Your dad grins. "Imperfect. Just how I like 'em."

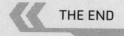

THE END

You start shouting again. "I'm not like the rest of you!"

Vwip! The disc pings off an embankment and whooshes straight at you. Before you can duck, it slices into your chest.

Your knees buckle and you drop to the ground. "Help me," you beg. But no one moves. They stand staring at you, mesmerized by the blood oozing out of your wound. Then it dawns on you: they've never seen blood before. Which also means they don't have the kinds of doctors you'd need.

You feel woozy as you try to stop the bleeding. But it's no use. This is . . .

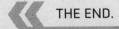

THE END.

You carefully creep to the doorway on the right, trying to avoid creaking floorboards. You want to hear what they're talking about before you introduce yourself. Being the son of Kevin Flynn doesn't quite have the pull you thought it would have here.

You lean against the doorjamb, listening.

"We must find Flynn," a voice growls. "We need him on our side."

"We don't even know if Flynn is alive," another voice protests. "Or if he'd be willing to join us."

"There are rumors," a female voice says. "The son is here. The Portal is alight."

"The rumors are true," you say, stepping into the room. "And I want to help."

Three startled programs stare at you: a burly man with a scar across his face, another equally huge guy, and a girl with a shaved head. Wow. What kind of group have you just joined?

"Grab him!" the scarred man shouts. "He'll rat us out to Clu."

"No!" you cry as they pounce. "I'm Sam Flynn! Kevin Flynn's son! I can prove it!"

Now they release you so quickly you fall to the floor with a thump.

You stay on the floor and show them your disc. Now they gaze at you with awe. Which feels a lot better than being attacked. But only barely. It's more than a little weird.

TURN TO PAGE 127

100

Your father. Kevin Flynn. Your *real* father—the age he would be now, had he never disappeared.

"Sam?" he says uncertainly.

"Long time," you reply.

"You have no idea," he says. He approaches you slowly, still staring at you as if he's not quite sure you're real. "You're here."

"Looks that way," you say.

He keeps smiling and then frowning, as if it's too much for him to take in. "How . . . ?"

"Alan came over—"

Now he nods. "Bradley. Alan Bradley."

"He got your page. I found the office under the arcade. You know the rest."

Puzzled, he looks at you. "A page . . ." He blinks a few times. "Dinner is soon. We'll continue then." He strides out of the room, leaving you with more questions than answers.

"You have to understand," Quorra says softly. "He thought he'd never see you again. This is very . . ." She shrugs.

"That's cool. I get it." You gaze down at your feet. You don't want her to see the emotions flooding through you.

She points you toward a room down the hallway. "Why don't you rest up before dinner?" she suggests.

You exit, grateful for time alone.

TURN TO PAGE 41

It looks as if no one ever patrols here. Broken glass and twisted metal litter the streets. A bitter wind howls through the crumbling buildings, cutting right through you. You want to get off the streets, warm up, and think. You duck inside an abandoned building.

Your eyes adjust slowly to the dim light. You don't know what used to be made here, but no one's been there in an awfully long time. Dust covers all the surfaces, and rusted machinery looms in the darkness like fossilized dinosaurs.

You find a spot that's out of the cold draft and sit. You hold your head in your hands, trying to put all the pieces of what you know together. Which isn't much. Least of all how to get yourself back home.

A sudden movement catches your attention. You're pretty sure someone just raced across the room and through a door on the left. Then you hear talking coming from the room on the right. Clearly, you aren't alone.

Should you find out who just ran through the space—and why they're in such a hurry? TURN TO PAGE 95.

Or do you want to find out who's talking and what they're talking about? TURN TO PAGE 99.

Finding your dad could take forever. And time is of the essence. Somehow *you* have to unite the rebels. Then, maybe your dad will come out of hiding voluntarily. But you need Bartik's help.

You make your way back to the dilapidated shack Bartik uses as rebel headquarters. You arrive during some kind of meeting.

"You're back!" Bartik crows as you step through the door. Then he looks puzzled. "You're alone?" His expression darkens with sorrow. "Was he . . . dead? Or did he refuse to come with you?"

You glance around the room full of fierce-looking men and women. For one second you consider lying to them, telling them that he didn't want to come. But that won't help the cause. So you take a deep breath and tell them the truth. "I realized by the time I found him it could be too late."

There's a general murmur of confusion and discontent. You hold up a hand. "Most of you don't know me," you say. "I'm Sam Flynn. Kevin Flynn's son. And I want to help overthrow Clu."

Now the room goes silent. You really hope you didn't make a big mistake.

Your jaw clenches and you hold your breath as they all stare at you. Bartik approaches you slowly. You prepare yourself for an attack.

TURN TO PAGE 118

"Cool!" Alex cries before Bartik can respond. "Rescuing Kevin Flynn. I'll be famous forever!"

"Slow down, kiddo," you tell him. "You'll be doing no rescuing. We need to get you back home."

Alex's eyes widen in fury. "No fair! You wouldn't even be here if it wasn't for me." His lower lip trembles as if he's about to cry.

"Hey, I'm not going to just send you packing," you tell him. "I need you to be my backup on the outside. In case something goes wrong."

He studies you suspiciously. "Really?"

"I swear," you say. "Your mission is critical." You find Alan's business card in your wallet and give it to Alex. "The minute you get home, call this guy. Tell him everything. He'll find a way to take out Clu—just in case we don't."

"The mini must go?" Veltor asks. He seems disappointed.

"We try to protect kids," you explain. "Otherwise they don't become adults. Now, how do we get him out of here?"

Bartik and Veltor exchange a look. "We're not sure," Bartik admits. "But the rumor is that Kevin Flynn came and went through the Portal on the island."

"So let's get to the Portal," you declare.

"We can't go with you," Bartik explains. "It's off the Grid."

You shrug. "That's where you said my dad is. So first I deliver Alex. Then I find my dad."

TURN TO PAGE 110

You can't leave your dad here. You've just found him again, and now you understand why he didn't return. You're sure you can get him to leave with you after a good night's sleep. The Portal has to stay open that long, right?

The next morning you wake up and find your dad doing yoga. Quorra is sipping tea and gazing out the window. Everything is so quiet you feel as if you should tiptoe.

"It's all right, Sam," your father says without looking at you. "Don't worry about making noise. It's all part of the experience."

"Can I talk to you?" you say.

"We're talking now," you father replies.

"I mean with us both right-side up."

"Don't limit yourself, man," your father says. But he gets out of his pose and sits in a lotus position.

"We really have to get out of here," you say. "There's a whole life—a whole *world* waiting for you outside. And for me."

"The world for me is the world within," your father says. "Inner space. So it doesn't matter if I'm in this safe house in the mountains of the Outlands or if I'm in the middle of the biggest city in the United States."

"It matters to *me*!" you exclaim, exasperated. You get up and stalk away from your dad. Otherwise you worry you might grab him and try to shake some sense into him.

TURN TO PAGE 91

Within minutes you've left the club and entered a subterranean level. "Your dad invented Tron?" Alex asks as you walk. "Why didn't you say so? He's like a total rock star!"

"I didn't think you were old enough to know who he was," you say, glancing at him. "He's been . . . gone, for a long time."

"I read all about him," Alex gushes. "Do you think he'll give me an autograph?"

"If we find him," you say. You follow Bartik and Veltor into a dilapidated shack with blacked-out windows. Bartik lights a small lamp, which casts everyone's face in shadow.

"I know why I'm looking for my dad," you say to Bartik as you settle into a rickety chair. "Why are you?"

"You really don't know?" Bartik asks. You shake your head. Then he launches into a story that makes your head swim. How your dad created this whole world, but one of his creations, Clu, managed to overthrow him. That Clu turned the place into a totalitarian nightmare where programs are hunted down and killed if Clu deems them "imperfect." And that there are signs that Clu is plotting something new. Something big.

"Which means now is the time to be rid of him. Once and for all," Bartik says. "If we can bring your father out of hiding, I know he'll be able to rally legions of programs to our cause."

"Do you have any idea where he is?" you ask.

Veltor sighs. "We suspect he's gone off-grid. Where no programs can go."

"But I can," you point out.

TURN TO PAGE 103

When you finally stop falling you find yourself in a strange landscape. It's very dark, except for occasional flashes of crackling light that trip across the blank terrain. Far in the distance in one direction is what looks like a massive city, and far off in the other direction you can see bursts of brightly colored lights on the horizon.

"We're in the computer!" Alex bounces around as if he's got springs on his feet. "I did it! I really did it! This is awesome! This is bigger than awesome! This is—"

"Would. You. Please. Just. Simmer. Down?" you say. Your brain feels like it's melting, and a crowing, hyper kid isn't helping.

"You're just jealous because I figured out how it worked and you didn't!" Alex brags.

"You having fun yet?" you say sarcastically. "Because you may have gotten us into this place, but now what?" You gesture broadly. "There's nothing to do out here but watch some flashes of light."

Alex frowns, and then his eyes well up.

Sheesh. "Hey, I didn't mean to upset you."

The kid flops to the ground. "I mess up everything!" he wails.

TURN TO PAGE 32

"Your disc," you say. "It's gone. That's a big problem, right?"

"Is it?" He throws out his hand to meet a control panel that emerges from the wall. He quickly punches in a code.

The floor beneath you opens! The elevator descends into an invisible sublevel. Here are the hidden wires, cables, pipes, and labyrinthine infrastructures from the Grid world. A place very few people other than your dad knows anything about.

The glass elevator shrieks to a stop. The doors open, but your father just stands there, not moving. You kneel beside Quorra who now lies motionless at your feet.

"I'm sorry. I screwed up," you say. If you had listened to your dad he wouldn't have lost his disc and Quorra wouldn't be injured. "We can go back to your safe house."

"This is the road we're on now," your father says.

"So what do we do?"

"We head to the Portal," he says.

You help him carry Quorra out of the elevator. Outside you see you've arrived at what looks like a wharf—only there's no water, just energy grids. A large cargo ship is floating in the air.

"A solar sailer," your dad murmurs, identifying the ship. "That's how we'll get to the Portal." Together you carry Quorra and sneak aboard the ship. Just as you lay Quorra on the platform, the ship breaks away from the Grid and unfurls its sails. It levels out like an airplane, heading out to sea.

TURN TO PAGE 28

Dashing over to the game, you duck down. Aha! You grab a pair of ankles and yank hard, pulling out a squirming, yelping kid.

"Leave me alone!" he squawks. He kicks out at you.

"Who are you? And what are you doing in here?" you demand.

"Let me go!" he yells. "Or I'll call the police!"

"*You'll* call the police? You're the one who's trespassing!" But you release him. He quickly scrambles to his feet.

"How did you send the page?" you ask.

He looks puzzled. "What page? You mean like from a book? I get into trouble if I tear up books. Ooh, I bet whoever sent you that page is going to get into big trouble."

You stare at him. "Not that kind of page. You know. Like from a phone."

Now the kid looks mad. He kicks the leg of a nearby game. "I don't have a stupid phone. It's no fair. All the other kids have them. My mom treats me like a big baby."

"Okay, okay!" you say, holding up your hands in surrender. Man, for someone so small he sure speaks in big chunks.

"Listen," you tell him with as much authority as you can muster without cracking yourself up, "If you leave now, I won't rat you out. No one's supposed to be here."

TURN TO PAGE 70

You drag Zuse over to the bar and haul him up onto it. You keep a strong grip on him—he's your ticket out.

You glance out at the crowd and see all eyes riveted on you. Good. Now if you can just make yourself heard over the pounding music! And keep Zuse from squirming away.

"Hey!" you shout.

"Hey!" they shout back.

That's weird. They're all mimicking you. Not just your words. Your every move—including each time you yank Zuse. They're grabbing their partners and jerking them. "What's wrong with them?" you ask Zuse.

He cackles. "They think this is the latest dance craze! We were in the middle of a dance contest when you made your untimely appearance." He starts to add little flourishes: a kick here, a toss of the head there. Everyone on the dance floor copies him.

"Listen to me!" you shout.

"Listen to me!" the crowd chants back.

"Give it up for our next dance champion!" Zuse shouts. They cheer.

"Shut up!"

« Should you toss Zuse into the crowd and announce his identity ON PAGE 67? »

« You don't want to lose your hold on Zuse—he's your bargaining chip. Shut down the music ON PAGE 73. »

You and Alex set out with a detailed map, a vehicle that has seen better days, and instructions. "According to Bartik, as long as that blue light is beaming, the Portal is open."

"Are you sure I can't stay?" Alex whines.

"Absolutely and totally sure," you reply.

You're able to use the vehicle for a while, but then, just as Bartik explained, it runs out of juice. That means you're now off-grid. The good thing is no one can look for you out here. The bad thing? Since none of the inhabitants can venture off-grid your map ends here. The pulsing Portal light is your only guide.

It feels like days before you finally reach the floating island that holds the Portal. Alex looks worried. "How's that supposed to get me home?"

You have no idea. But you don't want him to know that. "Remember when we came here? There was some kind of flashing light, right? So I guess we travel on beams of light or something." You glance down to see if he's buying this explanation.

He shrugs. "Makes sense." Without further adieu he steps up to the pulsating light. All his hair stands straight up. For one moment, you wonder if maybe you should go with him. Then you remember your father. Your mission.

Alex gives you a final wave, then shuts his eyes and leaps into the light. There's a blinding flash and a surge of energy so powerful it knocks you over.

You scramble back to your feet. Alex is gone. You hope he made it back okay. You wound up being really fond of the kid.

TURN TO PAGE 75

"Gotta go!" You grab Alex and spin around.

A beefy hand clamps down on your shoulder. "Run, Alex!" you shout. The boy takes off and disappears into the crowd.

Bartik spins you around roughly. "We need to know more about the small one," he says with a snarl. Then he calls over his shoulder. "Bring him back!"

"Leave the kid alone!" you shout. "He hasn't done anything wrong!"

A man dressed all in silver taps Bartik with a translucent staff. "Now, now, Bartik. Haven't I warned you before? Please take your fights outside. My insurance premiums keep going up!"

"Don't worry, Castor," Bartik says, but his eyes never leave your face. "I'll take this one to a nice quiet spot where we can talk."

"Hey! I'm innocent here," you tell Castor. "Don't let him—"

But Castor just shrugs and dances off into the crowd.

TURN TO PAGE 29

You wish you could spend more time with your father, but there's no way you're staying here. Once you're back home, you'll deal with Clu and help your dad from outside the system.

Your dad provides you with his bike and a fake disc—just in case you get stopped. He gives you a long, hard hug before you go. You're sorry he's not coming with you, but you're very glad you found him. You feel better than you have in a long time.

It's a long, hard ride to the Portal, and you have to keep stopping and hiding as patrols on foot and in the air blast their searchlights. But your dad gave you a great map that points out danger zones, good places to take cover, and shortcuts.

Not short enough. A few miles away from the Portal the light flickers wildly—then the beam blinks out. Completely.

You stand staring at the pitch black sky where just one minute ago there was an intense blue light. Too late. You waited too long. Your chance to get out is gone.

Now what?

You slowly turn your bike around back toward your dad's safe house. It may take you the rest of your days—and it seems like days can easily become years in this crazy place—but you vow you're going to find a way to overthrow Clu. This world will go back to being the brilliant, promising place your father originally created. And someday you'll escape.

With renewed purpose, you thunder along the Grid, knowing exactly where you're going.

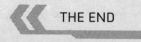

THE END

Jarvis holds up an ornate box and opens it. Clu pulls out a yellow baton. Then he offers the box to you. You remove a white baton. You inspect it and then wave it around, getting a feel for its weight.

"What do I do with this?" you ask.

Jarvis sneers at you. "I'll give you a hint. Not that."

Clu strides off as four programs emerge out of the Grid floor behind you. You recognize one of them as the kid from when you were held captive aboard the Recognizer. He's wearing aqua armor. The others are clad in purple, green, and blue. Are these your team members or are they your adversaries? And what are you supposed to do with the baton? Lead a marching band?

A loud whine emanating in the distance keeps you from asking the programs. You whip around and see two Sentries approaching rapidly on strange vehicles.

You remember these from the games your dad invented. Totally rocking motorcycles—Light Cycles, he called them.

"You've got no chance, user," the purple program snarls.

Okay, it's a good bet he's not on your side.

"Their cycles are faster than ours," the guy in green says. "Use the levels."

Levels? What levels?

TURN TO PAGE 59

You've seen what they do to programs here; you don't even want to think about what they'd do to *non*programs! And they'd probably have a whole lot of questions you won't be able to answer. Like how you got here.

"You can call me Mr. X," you declare. "I think an air of mystery is good for a gladiator like me!"

Okay, kind of lame. But it buys you a little time. You sidle toward the edge of the game platform as the people up in the ship confer. Maybe you can leap off and go into hiding—at least long enough to figure out what's going on. And how to get out of here!

No such luck. Before you get very far, Sentries roar out onto the platform and grab you. They haul you off to some kind of jail near the arena.

"What am I in for?" you ask. "Poor sportsmanship?"

The Sentries don't respond, they just toss you into a cell.

"Hey! I know my rights!" you shout. "I get one phone call. I demand to see my lawyer!"

The Sentries exit without a word. You slump onto the floor.

TURN TO PAGE 126

Your mission is to find your dad. So that's what you're going to do.

The wind picks up, chilling you to the bone. You jog toward the mountain, trying to get warm. You speed up, hoping the cliff face will give you some protection against the bitter cold.

When you reach the base of the mountain, an amazing thing happens—a door slides open! It must have motion-detecting devices installed. You dash inside, certain that you've stumbled onto your dad's hiding place. Who else could live out here? None of the inhabitants of this world can go off-grid.

Suddenly, alarms whoop and wail. "Intruder! Intruder!" an electronic voice booms. "Extermination in process!"

"No!" you scream. "It's me! Sam Flynn! I'm looking for my dad!"

The super-duper high-tech security system doesn't understand what you're saying. It just knows it's never seen you before.

And it has only one command: destroy.

THE END

You toss the keys into the garbage. Why should you waste your time looking for ghosts? Alan can have silly fantasies that Kevin Flynn has returned, but until your dad walks through your front door, you won't believe it.

The next morning you wake up late. You notice a bunch of voice-mail messages, but you don't bother checking them. Alan's visit put you in a funk.

You know exactly what will improve your mood. You climb aboard your motorcycle and peel out.

You speed into a deserted area of the city to a lot that's perfect for practicing. You do a few circles to warm up, making your loops tighter and tighter until you're practically horizontal. Then you alternate between riding only on your front tire and then only on your back tire. After several wheelies, you decide to go for a handstand on the handlebars.

You're up! You're in a handstand on the front of your bike. For one second. Then you completely wipe out. Luckily, you're wearing your safety gear.

You hear applause as you check to be sure you didn't break anything and glance up. It's a group of guys you've seen around before. Tyler, Kyle, and Luke. Bike freaks just like you.

"Looking good, Flynn," Tyler calls. He's the one who's a stuntman.

"Thanks!" you grin. You spend the rest of the afternoon trading moves.

You head for home feeling much better.

But once again, Alan is waiting.

TURN TO PAGE 27

This is not good. “We have to get your disc,” you say quietly.

“No,” your father says. “We beat him to the Portal. You can shut him down from the outside.”

“Even if I make it out, by the time I rewrite the code, they'll already be gone!” you argue. “Getting your disc is the only way.”

“He's right.” Quorra agrees.

You grin your thanks for her support. “You go find us some kind of transport out of here,” you tell your dad. “Quorra and I will take care of the disc.”

Your father stares at you a moment, as if he's finally starting to see you as the grown-up that you became while he was trapped in here. He smiles. “All right. There's an elevator toward the front which should bring you directly into Clu's throne room. The bridge—and the disc—are in the room beyond it.”

“Got it.” You nod sharply.

“Stay safe!” your father calls as you and Quorra race away.

No one notices you—they're all too focused on Clu. You easily make it to the elevator platform. “Be ready,” you warn Quorra.

The elevator opens and two Sentries immediately rush in, discs drawn.

TURN TO PAGE 53

No attack comes. Instead, Bartik picks you up in a bear hug. "You're right, Son of Flynn! Clu is on the move. Waiting for your father won't help us. But you!" He puts you back on the ground and clamps a beefy hand on your shoulder. "You will be our symbol!"

Phew. You're not sure how being a symbol will help, but at least they're not mad.

"Spread the word!" Bartik bellows to the assembled group. "Flynn—*our* Flynn," he adds with a wink to you, "is here and supports our cause. We attack the Rectifier tomorrow at dawn!"

The next morning you and hundreds of rebels hide near the opening of a massive cave. Programs have been entering and exiting nonstop. Bartik explains there's a military compound inside. That's your target.

It seems like a lost cause. You may have hundreds on your side, but Clu must have thousands. Plus major firepower.

"Are you sure this is the best way to go?" you ask Bartik. "Maybe we should try going one on one with Clu, rather than taking on an army."

"Have faith, Son of Flynn," he says.

You're dubious, but there's no backing out now.

"Come with me," Bartik says. Together you sneak up to a jagged ledge. Bartik raises his right arm. You do the same. "On my count," he says. "One . . . two . . . three."

"Now!" you and Bartik shout together, slicing your arms back down to your sides.

TURN TO PAGE 130

You decide to head for the city. Alex's excitement is contagious. Instead of feeling freaked out, you're psyched and ready to explore.

Even from this distance you can tell the scale of the city is huge. Full of skyscrapers—and if you squint you're pretty sure you can see space vehicles cruising through the steel and glass canyons.

"When do you think we can start playing?" Alex asks.

"As soon as we get somewhere, I suppose," you say letting the boy continue to think this is a game. "And figure out what exactly we're playing!"

You come to an area consisting of massive stadiums. Just beyond them lies the metropolis. You can hear the sound of a shouting crowd rising from the nearest arena. "Must be some kind of sporting event," you observe.

Alex frowns. "I'm not so good at sports."

"You don't know what kind of sports they play here," you point out.

"True," Alex concedes. "But I want to see what's on the top of that building." He points at the tallest structure in the city. It emits a pulsing light.

"That looks cool, too," you agree.

"So what should we do?" he asks.

Check out a nearby stadium ON PAGE 17.

Go deeper into the city ON PAGE 54.

You want to put distance between you and Clu as quickly as possible. You pound toward the bridge and the city. You hope you'll be able to lose yourself among the crowds in that glittering metropolis.

Suddenly, a blast of white light nearly blinds you. A Recognizer!

You dash to the side of the bridge. It's a *long* way down. But it's your best option. You slip through a space in the side rail. Once your feet hit the girder below, you slide, leap, and scramble down, down, down. You pass levels with ramps leading up and down, and other levels with brightly pulsating grid lights. You keep going—these upper levels probably have a fair amount of traffic. You need to find a far more deserted place to stop, regroup, and figure out your next move.

You continue down, your hands growing sore. Your shoulders burn from all the times you dangle before a stomach-clenching drop or hoist yourself up and over a girder. Is there even a bottom level in this world? Finally, you decide you've gone down far enough.

You duck under a girder and move cautiously onto the new level. You follow a ramp off the bridge and find yourself in a deserted, desolate area.

Perfect.

TURN TO PAGE 101

You ride in a circle, getting a feel for the bike.

Mistake! A disc whirs by your head, bounces off an edge of the platform, and zips back toward you. You swerve, and it passes close enough that you can feel its breeze.

There's no warming up in this game.

The crowd seems to like this new twist. They cheer loudly, stomp their feet, and hoot.

"The discs return to the thrower's hand," Alex says into your ear. "That gives you a couple of seconds before he gets his weapon back."

"Good to know," you say. You rev your bike and weave around the other player, creating a wall just like his.

Your opponent throws his disc again. This time you're ready for him.

"Hang on tight!" you tell Alex. You ride straight toward the other biker, even though you know his disc is hurtling right back to him. He holds his ground, waiting for the disc, certain you're going to crash into his wall.

Instead, you pop a wheelie and make a hard right. You narrowly whiz by his light wall and the disc misses you. Your opponent isn't so lucky. He smashes into your trailing light wall and derezzes.

"We win!" Alex pumps his fist in the air.

After that, you and Alex become the most popular stadium-game players. You're having so much fun, both of you forget to even try to get back home. Being champions rules!

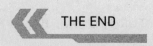

THE END

You race to the other side of the room, desperate to find an escape route. The guards crash through the skylight—and then through the glass floor into the club!

You scream as you fall through the floor with them—sending the club into total chaos. You hear shrieks and shouts over the throbbing music.

Bouncers unsheathe their discs and hurl them. You're not sure if they're going after the Black Guardsmen, you, or random programs. You make your way toward an exit. You spot the cool-as-a-cucumber DJ still in his spot. He throws down a thumping bass line and starts moving with the beat. But the bartender ducks below the bar for cover. Bartik, the revolutionary, jumps up from his seat.

"Resist!" Bartik shouts to the crowd. People cheer, and his gang whips out their discs and go after the Black Guard. With merciless efficiency, though, the Black Guard take out every one of them. While their attention is on Bartik's gang, you hurl yourself across the club floor, desperate to get to the exit.

A disc whizzes toward Bartik. He grabs a nearby program and uses him as a shield. *Bam!* The program derezzes. But before Bartik can pull out his own disc, he's hit. The revolutionary derezzes.

The guards are like heat-seeking missiles. They cut a deadly swath through the bar, taking out everyone and everything that comes between them and their target—you!

TURN TO PAGE 84

You can't leave the Rectifier—not without your dad, not after all you've gone through.

You turn and face the Sentries barreling toward you.

"Come on, Dad," you murmur. "Now would be a good time to make an appearance."

"This doesn't look good," Quorra observes.

"I have an idea." You wave your dad's disc at the Sentries. "I don't need this, but you do!" you shout. "Come any closer and I destroy it!"

This stops them. At least for a moment. You have no doubt that Clu will call your bluff. But he's not here. Yet.

"How's the gate?" you whisper to Quorra.

"Still closing," she whispers back. Then she clutches your shoulder. "I see him!"

You whirl around to see a strange-looking aircraft.

"Let's go!" You and Quorra race to the edge of the deck. The gate is just about to clang shut. You each somersault under the metal spikes as the Sentries thunder toward you.

It clangs shut—you on one side, Clu's army on the other.

Score!

TURN TO PAGE 138

"Kevin Flynn is out there somewhere," you hear a gruff voice say. "I'm sure of it."

You suddenly feel one hundred degrees colder. Then one hundred degrees hotter. Did you actually hear what you think you heard? This guy is talking about your father!

"Ow!" Alex yelps. "You're digging your fingers into me!"

"Sorry." You release your grip on Alex's shoulder. "I just need to listen to this."

Alex rolls his eyes and heaves a big sigh, but he stays put.

You lean toward the booth and see a large, intense guy with a diagonal scar across his face. He's talking to an equally tough-looking guy.

"The time is ripe, Bartik," one man says to the other. "If we find Flynn, you know he'll support us. Victory is assured."

"Not so fast, Veltor," Bartik says. "Remember what happened last time."

What happened last time? How is your father involved? You strain to hear them over the pumping music and the hum of hundreds of partying people.

Suddenly a lethal-looking circular object is at your throat. "We don't take kindly to eavesdroppers," Bartik snarls.

TURN TO PAGE 90

You look past the whimpering Jarvis and realize the elevator has been activated. Someone will be coming up here any minute. This can't be good.

Quorra's expression tells you she's realized the same thing. Her head whips around as she searches for another way out. But there's none.

You spot a weapons cache and hope you can find something more powerful than your discs.

"Tron Chutes!" Quorra exclaims when you throw her the gear. "Brilliant." You quickly strap one on.

Then she frowns. "They would be brilliant if we weren't sitting ducks trapped here in the bridge!"

The elevator doors begin to open. "Follow me!" you cry. You grab Quorra, and together you smash through the bridge window!

TURN TO PAGE 128

"You're in my spot," a voice snarls.

You look up and face the biggest guy you've ever seen—as if a sumo wrestler had been genetically combined with a basketball player. You can barely see the room beyond him.

"Sorry," you say, sliding over. "Didn't know this part of the floor was taken."

Mr. Big glares down at you. "What you in for?"

"Wouldn't give up my identity," you say. "Made the wrong people mad. It's like some kind of dictatorship out there."

The other prisoner's beady eyes glitter. He yanks you up to your feet. "We have more in common than you think."

"Oh, yeah?" You wriggle out of his clutches. "How so?"

He brings his enormous face close to yours. "Some of my buddies," he whispers hoarsely. "We're part of the underground. We're going to overthrow Clu."

Clu? Could he really mean the character your dad created all those years ago? He exists? And is he the person in charge? Or has this guy just been cooped up for too long?

"You in?" he asks. "We're working on our escape plans now. We'll put you to work right away. I'm the leader."

TURN TO PAGE 81

"So it is true," the man with the scar says as they help you back up to your feet. "I'm Bartik," he continues. He points at the other big guy. "That's Veltor, and she's Kindra."

The girl with the shaved head nods. "Welcome, Son of Flynn."

"Why do you need my dad?" you ask.

"He'll unite the factions to rise up against Clu," Bartik explains.

Veltor eyes you with satisfaction. "And you're just the person to convince him to join us."

You have a lot of questions, but if this group of rebels can help lead you to your father, you're in. Besides, from what you've seen so far, Clu isn't exactly a leader worth supporting.

"I have to get to work," Kindra says. "Let me know what happens."

After she leaves, Bartik and Veltor argue about strategy. You don't have much to contribute, since you're still trying to understand this crazy place. Ultimately they agree: Kevin Flynn is hiding off the Grid in an area known as the Outlands, and *you* should try to track him down.

It takes what feels like days, but they finally drop you off where they think your search should begin. Then they vanish back into the glittering Grid.

TURN TO PAGE 75

You plummet downward. Then you hit a button, and the winglike blades begin to whir and level you out.

The only problem—it's not as if you made a subtle exit. Sentries stream onto the deck from multiple directions, ready to fight.

You and Quorra zip toward the front of the Rectifier, desperately hoping to find your father waiting with an escape vehicle. You arrive at the very edge of the deck and power down, landing with a thud on the platform.

You scan the sky, but there's no sign of your dad. Now what?

Alarms wail and lights flash. "They must have discovered we took the disc!" you say.

"Lockdown!" a metallic voice booms. "Trap the intruders!"

"I'd say you're right about that," Quorra says.

You see a gate slowly descending at the entrance to the cave. Now what?

Maybe you should use the chutes to fly out of there and hope your dad will find you outside the cave. Too bad you don't know if he's still on the Rectifier.

Or you can try to hold your ground and hope that he arrives before the gate drops.

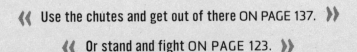

Use the chutes and get out of there ON PAGE 137.

Or stand and fight ON PAGE 123.

That bridge is just too precarious for you to make any surprise moves. You could send your dad plummeting to his death. Better to watch and wait. Your dad may have some ideas of his own.

"Clu did everything you asked," Rinzler says. "He took the system to its maximum potential. He was creating the perfect system!"

"The thing about perfection is that it's impossible—yet it's in front of us all the time," your father says philosophically. "He can't know that because I didn't when I created this world."

Rinzler eyes your father suspiciously, as if he doesn't trust—or understand—his compassion.

Then Rinzler suddenly springs forward and kicks Kevin hard in the stomach. Your father drops with a groan.

"No!" you shout.

TURN TO PAGE 80

130

With bloodcurdling war cries, the rebel forces charge into the cave. With the element of surprise, you get in the first strikes and take out program after program.

But soon their greater numbers turn the tide. Your comrades begin falling, and morale starts to fade.

Then a hush falls over the chaotic scene. You turn to see what has everyone's attention. A solitary figure stands at the entrance to the cave. He's backlit so you can't see his face, but everyone—Clu's men included—seems to be in awe of him.

He takes a step deeper into the cave and now you can see his face. It's your father!

"Cease your fighting!" he calls out.

People scatter. The rebels, Clu's army, everyone. You step forward. "Dad?"

He stares at you. He blinks several times as if he can't believe what he's seeing. "Sam? Is it really you? There were rumors, but I didn't trust them."

"I heard rumors about you, too," you say.

"You shouldn't be here," he warns. "It's much too dangerous."

"Can't do much about that right now, can I?" you say. "So how about we take care of this thing and worry about safety later."

He smiles slowly. "Okay, kid. Come on. We have an enemy to defeat."

You and your father march shoulder-to-shoulder, ready for the battle of your lives. Somehow, you know by joining forces, you're assured of victory in . . .

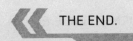

THE END.

You grab Alex and fling yourself off to the side. You land hard, but at least you avoid being run over.

"Get off me!" Alex squirms out from beneath you. "You're squashing me, dumbface."

"Hey! I just saved your life!" you snap.

But there's no time to argue. The motorcycles roar toward you again. You grab Alex's arm and drag him out of their path.

"Whoa! Cool!" Alex exclaims. You turn to see what he's watching.

Cool is right. The motorcycles are leaving trails of light behind them. This is very familiar. Then you remember. The Light Cycles! From your dad's game Tron! You have stumbled into a Light-Cycle match.

Suddenly a whirling disc flies by your head. You watch in horror as it slices off the head of one of the riders.

I don't remember that being part of the game, you think.

Then your eyes widen as you see the rider break into tiny pieces!

You glance down at Alex, hoping he's not too scared. To your shock, he's grinning broadly.

"I got my highest Tron score ever on a Light-Cycle game!" he cries. "That guy totally derezzed his opponent with his disc. This is the best day ever!"

You're not so sure about that.

TURN TO PAGE 134

132

Your dad knows how this place works a lot better than you do. If he says you can't get to the Portal in time, he's probably right. Then you'd still be stuck here—or a lot more vulnerable being out there with Clu searching for you.

But now that you've decided to stay, what is there to do?

Your dad starts teaching you some of the meditation techniques he's developed over the many, many years. Every day you learn something new that makes your head spin.

And speaking of spinning, you begin to master the twirling-data-streams trick you witnessed when you first arrived. Your dad is right. What's the point in getting worried about things you can't change. Better to go with the flow.

You go with the flow so much that you barely move anymore. You just allow the equations to float inside you. All that matters is inner space.

Four thousand years later, archaeology programs wanting to learn about the early days of the Grid discover your skeleton . . . still sitting in the same position.

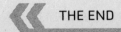

THE END

Your father abruptly leaves the room. Whatever happened to your dad in the past has made him reluctant to take any action. He just wants to leave the status quo intact. Even if the status quo bites.

The Portal is going to close soon. You have to make a decision. Do you get out now, leaving your father behind, before the Portal traps you here forever?

Or do you stay to convince your father to come with you? You don't know if you'll be able to maneuver in this crazy world on your own—and can you really just leave him here after finally finding him?

If you go now, TURN TO PAGE 88.

If you decide to wait until you can convince your dad to get out with you, TURN TO PAGE 104.

"Let's get up to the stands," you tell Alex, hauling him toward an opening in the arena. "We'll watch from up there." You know this is the safe, smart thing to do. But it would be pretty awesome to try out one of those souped-up vehicles.

Before you can make it off the platform, you hear a loud *whirr*—and the ground you're standing on starts to move! You and Alex revolve away from the exit and . . .

. . . come face-to-face with the remaining player on his Light Cycle. He circles around you and Alex, creating a light wall.

"I think we're about to play," you say.

"No problem," Alex says. "I'm an expert at this game."

"Alex, this isn't a video game—this is real life," you say. "And he's got a weapon and a bike!"

Alex cups his hands around his mouth. "Need a bike down here!"

To your shock, something drops from a craft hovering above the stadium. You hadn't noticed it before.

You dash over to retrieve it and discover it's a baton. As you run back to Alex it turns into a Light Cycle! You hop aboard and pick up Alex. He settles onto the seat behind you.

"Cool!" Alex cheers.

Now you might actually live through this. You hope.

TURN TO PAGE 121

You stand frozen for a moment, trying to figure out your next move. You hear a sound and turn. Quorra has come back and is hovering in the doorway. She is holding a hexagonal-shaped card.

"There's someone I once knew. . . ." She gives the card to you.

You gaze down at it. It's weathered and torn. There's a strange symbol on it and a map of the Grid.

"There was a program named Zuse who helped me once," she explains. "I haven't seen him in a long time, but they say he still runs the underground. Forges data for rogue programs, moves them around the Grid. They say he can get anyone anywhere."

"How do I find him?" you ask.

She nods at the card. "That's his sector. Make it there alive and he'll find you."

Her message delivered, she quickly vanishes back into her room.

It's time to go.

TURN TO PAGE 64

You reach for your disc, ready to fight Rinzler. But your father clamps his hand on your arm. “No, son. This is mine.”

You and Quorra watch anxiously as your father meets the warrior in the middle of the swaying, derezzing bridge.

Your stomach clenches. You're not sure who will be the victor in this battle.

Maybe you should go after Rinzler while he's distracted by your dad. But would that put your father in more danger?

No matter what you choose to do you need to decide fast. The Portal is closing!

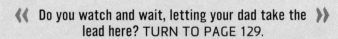

Do you watch and wait, letting your dad take the lead here? TURN TO PAGE 129.

Or do you try to derrezz Rinzler ON PAGE 82?

You power up your chutes and together you zip off the deck. Unfortunately, flying in formation above the vast Rectifier makes you a perfect target.

Within seconds an entire army of programs shoot you down.

Well, you think as you fall, at least you won't live to see Clu take over the world.

THE END

Luckily, you're still wearing your Tron Chutes. You hit the controls and land in the vehicle your dad is commandeering. Once you and Quorra crawl inside, your dad peels away from the cave.

You see the gate rising already—any minute now the Sentries will come after you.

"It's all yours," your dad says to Quorra. He moves out of the way as she slides into the driver's seat. He points toward the pillar of light. "Got a great landmark to navigate by."

"To the Portal!" Quorra declares.

You hand your father his disc. "Try to hang on to this," you joke. "I have a feeling you're going to need it."

He ruffles your hair as if you were seven years old again. "Thanks, kid."

The vehicle lurches and shudders. "What's happening?" you ask.

"I can't steer!" Quorra cries.

"Is it Clu?" you ask your dad. "Could he be doing something?

Your father shakes his head. "It's the Portal. The energy around it is very unstable."

Great. You escaped from Clu and his henchmen only to have the Portal almost kill you!

TURN TO PAGE 52